Speed Reading: Unlock Your Brain's Potential

Master the Art of Speed Reading and Boost Your Learning Efficiency

Emily Hayes

Table of Contents

INTRODUCTION

Welcome to "Speed Reading: Unlock Your Brain's Potential: Master the Art of Speed Reading and Boost Your Learning Efficiency." In a world where information flows at an unprecedented pace, reading swiftly and comprehending effectively is a powerful skill. This book is designed to guide you on a journey to enhance your reading speed while maintaining or improving your understanding of the material. Whether you're a student striving to manage a heavy workload, a professional seeking to stay ahead in your field, or a lifelong learner eager to consume more knowledge, mastering speed reading can transform your life.

We begin by debunking common myths about speed reading, setting the stage for a science-based approach emphasizing speed and comprehension. By understanding the intricacies of the reading process, identifying and overcoming poor reading habits, and creating an optimal environment for learning, you'll be equipped with the skills to read faster without sacrificing comprehension. The benefits of these techniques are not just theoretical, but practical and applicable to your everyday life.

This book also delves into the application of speed reading across various contexts—academic, professional, and leisure—ensuring that you can apply these techniques to any reading material. With real-life case studies, expert insights, and a focus on boosting overall learning efficiency, this guide offers a comprehensive pathway to unlocking your brain's potential. Embark on this journey with us and transform how you read, learn, and engage with the world.

CHAPTER I

Getting To Know Speed Reading

The Importance of Reading Speed

The ability to read is a fundamental life skill that significantly impacts our capacity to learn, digest information, and be effective in many different areas. The rate at which a person reads can dramatically influence these domains, including professional effectiveness, personal growth, and academic achievement. In today's information-driven society, being able to read rapidly and comprehend well is not only a helpful talent but also essential. Enriched with real-life examples, this section examines the significance of reading speed and how it affects learning and productivity. It also provides examples from everyday life and personal experiences to bolster its arguments.

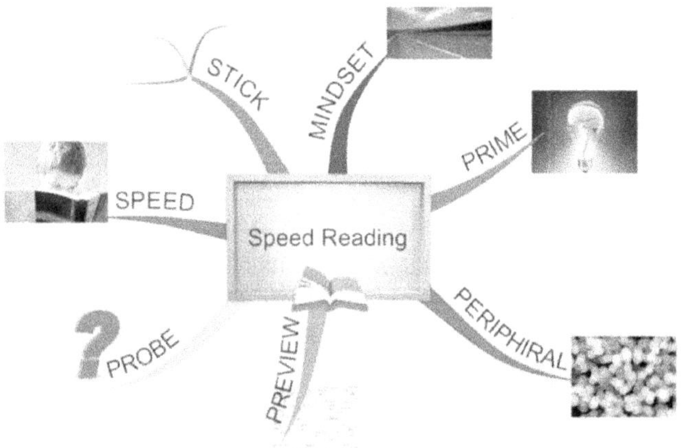

First, reading speed has a direct impact on how well students learn. Students in an academic setting frequently have to read a lot of material in a short amount of time. Faster readers without sacrificing comprehension have a significant advantage since they can read more material in less time. They can comprehend challenging ideas more quickly, combine knowledge from many sources, and do well on tests and tasks. If a student can read a chapter in a textbook in half the time it takes others, for instance, they can use that extra time to check their notes, participate in class discussions, or look for other resources, which will help them grasp the content better.

Furthermore, reading speed is essential in professional contexts where information must be digested fast and precisely. Emails, reports, proposals, and papers that need quick reading and comprehension are sent daily to professionals. A quick reader can effectively manage this flood, who can act quickly on pressing problems, and make judgments more quickly. Better job performance and career advancement may result from this talent. A lawyer, for example, can better prepare for court by reading and understanding case files fast, while a corporate executive can make timely strategic judgments by quickly absorbing market reports.

Increased reading speed has advantages for career and academic pursuits, as well as increased productivity and personal development. Many people aim to read more books, articles, and other written materials to expand their knowledge and abilities. Their ability to read more quickly enables individuals to take in more information in less time, which promotes lifelong learning and personal growth. An enthusiastic reader who increases their reading pace, for instance, can go deeper into a greater variety of subjects and genres and acquire a variety of viewpoints and ideas. Knowledge expansion like this can improve critical thinking, creativity, and general intellectual development.

Examples from real life further highlight how reading speed can have a transforming effect. Let us examine the situation of Anne, a history major at the university. At first, Anne needed help to meet the demanding reading requirements of her classes. She often felt overburdened and tired after spending hours reading textbooks and articles. Ann decided to take a speed reading course because she wanted to get better. She could read much more quickly by using new strategies and increasing her practice. As a result, Anne could better organize her schoolwork and make time for readings that deepened her comprehension of historical settings. She saw an improvement in her academic standing and graduated with honors, mainly attributing her accomplishment to her increased reading abilities.

Regarding the professional sphere, let's examine Mark's experience as a project manager at a technology company. Mark's job description included daily assessment of many project ideas, technical documents, and team reports. At first, Mark was overwhelmed by the necessary reading, and he frequently stayed late to finish his assignments. He committed time to increasing his reading speed using a variety of workouts and techniques after realizing that something needed to change. Due to this change, Mark could make better judgments more quickly, prioritize work more effectively, and digest information more quickly. Mark's increased productivity was not ignored; he was given multiple promotions and gained recognition for his keen analytical abilities and effortless management of challenging assignments.

Reading speed has a significant influence on hobbies and personal endeavors as well. Consider Susan, a businesswoman and mother of two. Susan had always loved to read, but she found it challenging to indulge her enthusiasm for literature while juggling her obligations in her personal and professional life. Susan's restricted free time allowed her to read more books, so she learned fast reading techniques. This gave her the much-needed leisure and fun she required and insightful knowledge and inspiration for her business endeavors. Susan could innovate in her firm and achieve growth and success because of the knowledge she got from reading various resources.

Increased reading speed has advantages beyond personal achievement and impacts the more extensive educational and professional environments. Schools that strongly emphasize reading instruction can turn out students who are more capable and self-assured. With their increased reading and comprehension speed, these students will be better able to contribute to their academic disciplines and future employment. Similarly, companies may improve productivity, innovation, and competitive advantage by investing in their workforce's reading and comprehension abilities.

Notwithstanding these benefits, it's crucial to remember that understanding shouldn't be sacrificed for reading speed. Both factors must be balanced for effective speed reading, a concept we will delve into, to guarantee that the reader remembers and comprehends the content. To attain this equilibrium, strategies including chunking, skimming, and using contextual signals can be useful. Furthermore, consistent practice combined with slow, steady speed increases can result in long-lasting gains without sacrificing comprehension.

In summary, the significance of reading speed cannot be emphasized enough. It has a major effect on professional productivity, personal growth, and learning efficiency. We learn how improved reading speed may result in scholastic success, job advancement, and richer personal lives through the examples of people like Susan, Mark, and Anne. However, it's crucial to remember that understanding shouldn't be sacrificed for reading speed. Both factors must be balanced for effective speed reading to guarantee that the reader remembers and comprehends the content. The capacity to read swiftly and efficiently will always be an important and empowering trait as we continue to adjust to the demands of modern life.

Debunking Myths About Speed Reading

For a considerable time now, speed reading has been a subject of interest and debate, drawing proponents who assert remarkable advantages and detractors who cast doubt on its veracity. Like many abilities that offer substantial benefits, there are a lot of myths and misconceptions about rapid reading. In addition to presenting the facts of speed reading and dispelling some of these widespread misconceptions, this section fairly assesses what is practically achievable.

The idea that anyone can read thousands of words per minute while still having excellent comprehension is one of the most widespread misconceptions regarding speed reading. Ads for books and classes on speed reading frequently make extraordinary claims about how quickly one can understand complex texts or finish a novel in only a few minutes. Nonetheless, research continuously demonstrates that the human brain's capacity to process information quickly without sacrificing comprehension has limits. Although there is a limit to how fast one can read, the extreme claims of reading at superhuman rates are frequently incorrect and vastly overstated.

Another widespread misunderstanding is that reading faster means glancing at the text more quickly. Compelling speed reading, however, calls for cognitive skills to improve comprehension and retention in addition to quick eye movements. Critical components of speed reading include strategies like chunking, which involves readers grouping words into meaningful pieces, limiting subvocalization, or the internal voice that happens while reading. Although they take practice and skill development, these strategies aid readers in processing information more quickly. These strategies are necessary for rapidly moving your eyes to improve comprehension and memory.

Another element commonly misinterpreted in the context of fast reading is subvocalization, or the inner voice we frequently hear when reading. Some proponents of speed reading contend that the secret to reading more quickly is avoiding subvocalization. That being said, this is not true. Although reading speed can be increased by lessening subvocalization, eliminating it is not feasible or desirable. Subvocalization is essential for understanding, particularly when reading complex or novel content. The intention is to reduce superfluous subvocalization to accelerate reading while preserving its ability to support comprehension when essential.

The idea that speed reading compromises comprehension in favor of speed is a major fallacy. Detractors contend that reading more quickly invariably equates to poorer comprehension. Although there is a trade-off between comprehension and speed, it could be more apparent. Studies reveal that people can improve their reading speed by appropriate methods and repetition without appreciably sacrificing comprehension. Competent speed readers can read more quickly without losing sight of vital information because they can rapidly recognize important details, deduce context, and make intelligent assumptions about the text.

The idea that rapid reading is best suited for reading light fiction or non-technical literature is another misconception. This misperception needs to recognize how adaptable speed reading strategies are to different kinds of books. For example, rapid reading techniques can be instrumental when skimming academic papers to find pertinent passages, skimming reports in a work environment, or scanning news articles to stay current on current events. Although reading thick and highly technical material may necessitate a slower, more deliberate pace, speed reading techniques can still benefit overall productivity and facilitate information processing.

Another common misconception about speed reading is that it's an inherent skill only a select few can acquire. This misconception can deter people from increasing their reading speed because they believe they are not naturally gifted with it. However, with the proper instruction and practice, rapid reading is a skill that can be acquired. Like picking up a musical instrument or becoming an expert athlete, increasing reading speed calls for commitment, the appropriate methods, and regular practice. With the correct technique and effort, most people can dramatically improve their reading comprehension and speed.

Another fallacy that has to be dispelled is the idea that rapid reading is a relatively new phenomenon. Although the phrase "speed reading" and the organized classes that teach it have gained popularity recently, the ideas behind the ability are not. Many techniques to increase reading proficiency have been investigated throughout history. For instance, to read and comprehend books faster, scholars in antiquity employed various strategies. Our knowledge of cognitive processes and the creation of systematic methods for teaching and practicing speed reading have changed.

Speed reading and its potential are better understood in light of scientific studies. Eye-tracking studies, for instance, have revealed that adept speed readers move their eyes more efficiently than typical readers. They fixate on words for shorter periods and do fewer regressions or backward eye movements. They can scan more content and retain comprehension because of their efficiency. Furthermore, research on brain imaging has shown that speed readers might employ several cognitive techniques to read more rapidly, such as improved word anticipation and successful context integration.

Beyond just being efficient, fast reading can also improve cognitive functioning. Speed reading is a mentally taxing activity that can enhance cognitive flexibility and processing speed. This is comparable to how consistent exercise increases physical fitness. Speed readers can improve their mental agility by forcing their brains to comprehend information more quickly. This can help them in many areas of life, such as decision-making and problem-solving.

Even while speed reading has advantages and possibilities, having reasonable expectations is crucial. While reading speed may be significantly increased, doing so takes patience, practice, and the right approach. Focusing too much on speed alone can be detrimental, disregarding comprehension and retention. Achieving a balance between speed and comprehension through compelling speed reading enables readers to process and retain material more quickly.

To sum up, fast reading is a valuable talent that can significantly improve learning and productivity if it is learned and performed correctly. A more accurate and helpful understanding of speed reading is made possible by dispelling common misconceptions, such as superhuman reading speeds, reducing the talent for rapid eye movements, and the belief that it is exclusively helpful for particular reading content. Studies have demonstrated that chunking and reducing subvocalization can increase reading comprehension and speed. Acknowledging speed reading as a trainable ability instead of an innate talent allows people to approach the practice with a balanced mindset and reasonable objectives, enabling them to reap the complete advantages of this proper cognitive function.

Overview of the Book

The complete manual "Speed Reading: Unlock Your Brain's Potential: Master the Art of Speed Reading and Boost Your Learning Efficiency" aims to revolutionize how you read, absorb, and assimilate data. With its careful organization, the book offers readers scientific insights, valuable strategies, and real-world applications of speed reading—all of which contribute to a well-rounded approach to reading faster without sacrificing understanding. This article offers a thorough synopsis of the book's contents and advantages, outlining what readers may anticipate learning from each chapter.

Chapter 1 of the book is titled " Getting To Know Speed Reading." This chapter emphasizes the necessity of reading speed in today's fast-paced world, which sets the scene. It discusses how reading speed affects learning and productivity, illuminating its views with anecdotes from the author's life and actual situations. Along with dispelling popular misconceptions regarding speed reading, the chapter offers a practical summary of what is feasible. Readers will have a clear idea of the book's goals and how fast reading can change their lives by the end of this chapter.

The second chapter, "Understanding the Reading Process," explores the physiological and cognitive elements. It describes how humans read, emphasizing eye movements, fixations, and the function of the brain in text processing. This chapter lists typical reading errors like regression and subvocalization and provides tips on how to fix them. It also emphasizes how crucial it is to balance comprehension and speed so that readers can rapidly grasp the information they read. Readers are better prepared for the practical methods covered in later chapters by this core knowledge.

The emphasis moves to creating the ideal environment for practicing speed reading in Chapter 3, "Preparing for Speed Reading." Readers learn to set realistic goals to establish the best possible reading environment. The chapter stresses the value of reducing outside distractions and becoming physically and psychologically ready for reading. It also introduces critical resources and tools, like suggested books, apps, and gadgets for quick reading. Readers will have all the tools they need to start their speed reading journey by the end of this chapter.

The book's central chapter, "Techniques for Speed Reading," offers doable methods for accelerating reading speed. It includes sophisticated strategies like chunking words, employing peripheral vision, and more fundamental ones like scanning and skimming. Readers can practice these strategies using exercises and step-by-step directions provided in the chapter. By regularly using these techniques, readers can acquire the speed reading abilities necessary to increase reading speed without compromising comprehension. The practical nature of this chapter encourages practice and active engagement.

Chapter 5, "Building Speed Reading Skills," expands on previously covered methods and concentrates on skill development. It offers exercises to strengthen vocabulary and comprehension, lessen regression, and manage eye movements. To assist readers in breaking through obstacles and moving forward, the chapter also provides ways for progressively increasing reading speed. Readers can develop their speed reading skills methodically and monitor their progress over time by adhering to the advice provided in this chapter.

In Chapter 6, "Speed Reading in Different Contexts," the use of speed reading strategies is examined in several situations. It deals with academic reading and offers tips for effectively managing study materials, research papers, and textbooks. The chapter also discusses professional reading and provides advice on handling materials linked to the workplace, including memoranda, reports, and emails. It also covers leisure reading, ensuring readers can utilize rapid reading strategies for fiction and non-fiction and still appreciate the material. The adaptability of fast reading and its applicability to various facets of life are illustrated in this chapter.

In Chapter 7, "Boosting Learning Efficiency," fast reading is combined with other learning strategies to improve cognitive performance. It presents cognitive strategies for improved recall, including mnemonics and memory procedures. The chapter also looks at how to use the SQ3R method, mind mapping, and other study techniques in addition to fast reading. A multimodal approach to learning can help readers learn more effectively and retain it longer. This chapter encourages readers to hone their talents by emphasizing lifelong learning and ongoing progress.

Chapter 8, "Overcoming Challenges in Speed Reading," advises dealing with typical roadblocks during speed reading. The chapter includes techniques for handling challenging texts and new subjects, preventing eye strain and weariness, and maintaining motivation. It also emphasizes the value of endurance and patience, reminding readers that rapid reading is a talent that needs constant work and commitment. Readers can keep progressing and getting better by comprehending and conquering these obstacles.

In Chapter 9, "Case Studies and Success Stories," people who have succeeded with speed reading are profiled. Expert interviews on speed reading, trainers' and writers' perspectives, and anecdotes from professionals, students, and voracious readers are all featured in this chapter. These case studies highlight helpful advice and critical takeaways, highlighting the advantages of fast reading in many settings. Readers can obtain the confidence and drive to use speed reading strategies in their own lives by taking inspiration from these success tales.

Chapter 10, "Next Steps To Speed Reading," summarizes the book's main ideas and tactics. It invites readers to evaluate their development and accomplishments, make long-term plans for speed reading, and establish objectives for the future. The chapter concludes with inspirational words to encourage readers to keep getting better. It highlights the value of lifetime learning and constant practice. Readers will have a clear plan for maintaining and improving their speed reading abilities by the end of this chapter, allowing them to continue reaping the benefits of this invaluable talent.

The thorough manual "Speed Reading: Unlock Your Brain's Potential: Master the Art of Speed Reading and Boost Your Learning Efficiency" gives readers the information and abilities they need to change how they read. Every chapter builds upon the one before it, offering a systematic and planned way to become an expert speed reader. The book provides a comprehensive approach to speed reading, covering everything from comprehending the cognitive components of reading to using advanced strategies and conquering obstacles. Readers can enhance their learning effectiveness, unleash the full potential of their brains, and become more competent and confident in navigating the information-rich world by heeding the advice in this book.

CHAPTER II

Understanding the Reading Process

How We Read

The cognitive reading process is multifaceted, requiring precise synchronization of multiple brain processes with motor actions. Examining the fundamental mechanisms, especially eye movements and fixations, essential elements of reading, is necessary to comprehend how humans read. This section explores the cognitive process of reading, concentrating on the function of fixations and eye movements in our capacity to interpret and understand written language.

Reading is fundamentally the act of deriving meaning from written symbols. The eyes are the first organs involved in this process, gathering the visual data of letters and words. In reality, the eyes move in a sequence of abrupt, jerky movements called saccades, as opposed to the conventional notion of smooth, continuous movement. Saccades are quick eye movements three to four times a second and broken up by fixations, which are quick bursts of steadiness. The eyes travel quickly from one spot to another during a saccade, sometimes covering many words or numerous letters. Crucially, the brain receives and processes visual input only during fixations; no visual information is processed during saccades.

Fixations, ranging from 200 to 500 milliseconds, are periods when the eyes are comparatively still. The visual system gathers specific information from the text during these fixations. After that, the brain translates these images into meaningful words by interpreting the data. Depending on the reader's ability level, the text's complexity, and the reading goal, fixations differ in length and frequency. Longer saccades and shorter fixations are characteristics of skilled readers that enable them to process text faster. On the other hand, because they take longer to comprehend each word, inexperienced readers or those reading complex material may display longer fixations and shorter saccades.

Saccades and fixations follow a very deliberate, well-planned pattern. Instead of focusing on every word, readers frequently bypass short, common words like "the" and "and" in favor of longer, more informative content terms. This focused concentration maximizes the effectiveness of reading. Furthermore, proficient readers can anticipate and prepare for the subsequent fixation by using their peripheral vision to gather preparatory information about impending words. Keeping a fluid and adequate reading flow depends on your capacity to assimilate information from the periphery.

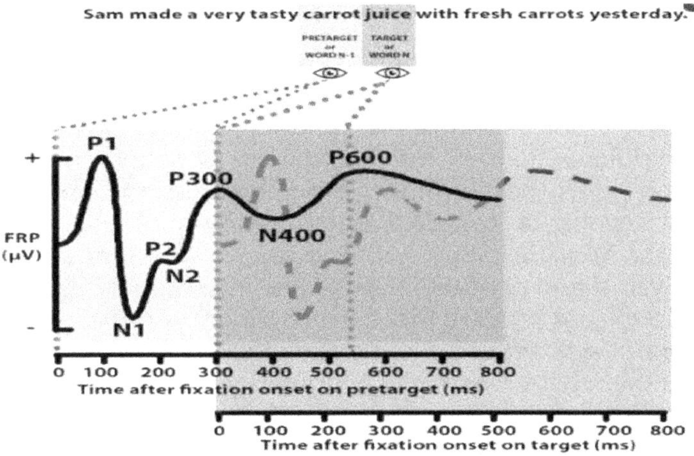

Regression, sometimes known as backward saccades, is crucial to eye movements during reading. Regressions happen when the eyes go back to review something that has already been read. Regressions are a regular aspect of reading and can happen for several reasons, even though they are frequently interpreted as an indication of difficulty or misunderstanding. These could occur when a reader comes across a complex or confusing sentence, needs to know the definition of a term they've already read, or just gets disoriented in the text. Regressions are a valuable tool for proficient readers to ensure they have digested the content correctly and improve comprehension.

Reading is a cognitive process involving more than eye movements and fixations. After being collected during fixations, visual information is sent to the brain's visual cortex for preliminary processing. The visual cortex converts letters and words into distinguishable language units by decoding their patterns and shapes. The brain's language centers, mainly found in the left hemisphere, receive this information and process it further to derive meaning. Language comprehension and production rely heavily on areas like Wernicke's and Broca's, which make it easier to understand syntax, semantics, and context.

Working memory, attention, and prior knowledge are only a few cognitive processes that must be integrated for reading comprehension. Readers may keep and manipulate textual information in working memory, which helps them connect new and existing knowledge and develop a cohesive understanding of the subject matter. While existing knowledge offers a foundation for analyzing and contextualizing new information, attention ensures that readers focus on pertinent information and filter out distractions. Fluent and efficient reading is made possible by the seamless cooperation of these cognitive processes.

A reader's level of expertise, the text's complexity, and the reading activity can all impact how well their eye movements and fixations move. Skilled readers, for example, usually have more efficient eye movements, with longer saccades, shorter fixations, and fewer regressions. Additionally, they are more adept at foreseeing words and phrases using contextual clues and past knowledge, speeding up the reading process. On the other hand, ineffective eye movement patterns, like prolonged fixations, brief saccades, and numerous regressions, make it difficult for beginning readers or people with reading issues to read fluently and comprehend what they read.

Eye movement patterns are significantly influenced by text complexity as well. Readers typically read simple, well-known texts with more fluid eye movements and fewer fixations and regressions. However, readers may need to slow down when text complexity rises due to more complex language, complicated syntax, and dense material. This will cause longer fixations and more regressions. Though at a slower speed, this modification enables readers to comprehend and assimilate the more complicated material fully.

The reading activity itself also influences eye movements and fixations. For instance, reading for pleasure—like reading a novel—often requires a fluid, more laid-back reading style with longer saccades and fewer regressions. On the other hand, reading for research or professional purposes, where understanding and remembering specific details are essential, can call for a more deliberate and attentive reading style, marked by fewer fixations and more regressions. The degree of cognitive engagement and processing required for various reading activities determines eye movement patterns.

Technological developments in eye tracking have yielded significant insights into the nuances of fixations and eye movements during reading. Researchers can examine reading behavior in depth thanks to eye trackers, which employ infrared light to identify and record eye movements precisely. These studies have demonstrated how eye movement patterns vary and adapt to various readers, texts, and tasks. Additionally, they have emphasized how crucial effective eye motions are to read fluently and effectively.

Optimizing eye movement patterns is frequently the primary goal of training programs and therapies to enhance reading abilities. Methods like visual tracking exercises, guided practice, and speed reading classes are designed to decrease needless regressions, increase the use of peripheral vision, and improve the efficiency of saccades and fixations. Through these programs, readers can learn more effective eye movement techniques to increase their reading speed, comprehension, and fluency.

In summary, the cognitive process of reading involves a dynamic and intricate interaction between the brain's functions, fixations, and eye movements. The visual system uses saccades and fixations as essential building blocks to collect and interpret information from printed text. Fluent and effective reading needs efficient eye movement patterns, typified by ideal fixations, well-timed saccades, and efficient use of peripheral vision. Knowing how eye movements and fixations affect reading gives essential insights into the complexities of this crucial cognitive ability. It opens up possibilities for improving reading proficiency through focused practice and instruction.

Common Reading Habits

The ability to read well significantly impacts our capacity for knowledge acquisition, literary engagement, and effective communication. Even with this, many readers form bad habits that can impair their reading understanding and effectiveness. Subvocalization, regression, and fixation are three of these tendencies that are particularly prevalent. Reading enjoyment and proficiency can be significantly increased by being aware of these habits, their consequences, and effective ways to overcome them.

The practice of mentally saying words aloud while reading is known as subvocalization. Early reading education is the source of this habit, as it teaches youngsters to sound out words to comprehend their pronunciation and meaning. For more proficient readers, subvocalization becomes a barrier, even though it can be helpful for beginner readers. Reading becomes slower when one subvocalizes since the mind processes text much more quickly than when someone speaks silently. As a result, subvocalizers frequently read at a speed comparable to their speaking speed, which is much slower than their optimal reading speed.

Subvocalization's main drawback is that it restricts how much information a reader can receive at once. A subvocalizer will probably read in the 150–200 word per minute range because this is the average speaking rate. Competent silent readers, on the other hand, can read between 300 and 500 words per minute. This disparity suggests that subvocalization can reduce reading comprehension by at least half. Moreover, subvocalization may diminish overall understanding. By concentrating on word pronunciation, readers may devote less mental energy to comprehending and applying the information, which could result in skimming the text and retaining less.

Readers might use many ways to deal with subvocalization. One efficient way is to practice speed reading strategies, such as chunking, which involves grouping words or sentences and reading them as a single unit. This method lessens the propensity to subvocalize words separately. Another technique is to lead the reader's eyes swiftly across the text using a pen or pointer to minimize subvocalization and encourage a faster reading rate. Furthermore, readers can deliberately direct their attention from pronunciation to comprehension by picturing the text's meaning rather than its sound.

Another typical barrier to good reading is regression or the practice of repeatedly reading a material. Regression can sometimes help explain complex or unclear portions, but it is a sign of insecurity or inattention when it occurs frequently. Regressions frequently break the reading flow, resulting in reduced reading efficiency and fragmented comprehension. Distractions and lack of concentration often worsen this behavior, making readers forget their position and keep returning to understand what they've read.

Regression has detrimental effects that go beyond slower reading. Because of the monotonous nature of reading can lead to a vicious cycle of dissatisfaction and low motivation in readers. This can eventually undermine self-esteem and lessen the enjoyment of reading. Readers can learn techniques to improve focus and keep a consistent reading pace to reduce relapse. Previewing the text before reading it is a valuable strategy that entails quickly scanning the headings, subheadings, and summaries to obtain a general idea of the content. As a mental framework for the content, this initial comprehension can lessen the need for regressions.

Engaging in active reading is another helpful strategy. Asking questions, providing summaries, and making predictions about the material are all examples of active reading. Through active engagement with the information, readers can improve their focus and understanding, reducing the chance of regressions. Moreover, establishing clear reading objectives, like finishing a particular number of pages in time, can promote constant advancement and reduce needless rereading.

Fixation is the third typical reading habit that might reduce reading efficiency. Fixation is the tendency to focus on single words or small groups of words for extended periods. Although fixations are a standard reading, prolonged or excessive fixations indicate ineffective eye movement and processing. 90% of the words in a text are fixed in the eyes of the ordinary reader, who spends too much time on each fixation, slowing reading comprehension and decreasing reading speed.

Overemphasis on word-by-word reading and unfamiliarity with effective reading techniques are the usual causes of excessive focus. When readers concentrate on specific words rather than the larger context and flow of the text, it might result in a fragmented understanding of the text. Readers can train their eyes to move across the text more smoothly and efficiently to combat fixation. Fixation time can be shortened using strategies like peripheral vision training, in which readers practice word recognition and processing without looking at the text directly.

Reading longer passages of text aloud and progressively increasing the amount of information processed each fixation is another helpful tactic. Exercises that promote reading passages or groups of words at once instead of focusing on each word separately can help achieve this. Additionally, developing smoother and more effective eye motions can be aided by using devices like pacemakers, which keep the eyes at a constant tempo.

Frequent reading habits like subvocalization, regression, and focus can seriously hinder reading comprehension and efficiency. Readers can improve their reading ability and get more enjoyment by identifying and changing these habits. Overcoming these tendencies can result in more productive and pleasurable reading by practicing strategies like active reading exercises, speed reading techniques, and practical eye movement training. Readers can interact with a wider variety of texts and gain a deeper awareness of the world by developing these skills, allowing them to reach their full reading potential.

The Role of Comprehension

Reading is a complex skill that requires word recognition, comprehension, and memory of the material being read. For many, the main difficulty is balancing reading comprehension and speed. Although reading rapidly can boost productivity, comprehension of the content is frequently sacrificed. On the other hand, reading might become a frustrating crawl if comprehension is the only thing on your mind. Therefore, for anyone wishing to improve their reading competence and general learning experience, knowing strategies for maintaining comprehension at increased reading rates is essential.

Reading comprehension and speed are frequently viewed as mutually exclusive. Advocates of speed reading contend that reading at a rate far faster than the average—between 200 and 300 words per minute—can be done without sacrificing comprehension. Critics counter that reading quickly can result in superficial comprehension and poor memory recall of the content. It is crucial to comprehend the cognitive processes associated with reading and to use tactics that promote speed and understanding to strike a balance between these two factors.

Decoding, or converting text into intelligible language, is one of the primary cognitive functions of reading. When a reader is adept, decoding becomes automatic, freeing up more cognitive resources for comprehension. On the other hand, reading quickly can overload the brain, which lowers comprehension. Therefore, increasing one's vocabulary and background knowledge is a valuable strategy to balance speed and comprehension. An extensive vocabulary makes it possible for readers to identify terms more quickly, and a rich history gives new material context and makes it easier to understand. By improving these fundamental abilities, readers may interpret material more quickly and effectively, which frees up mental energy for understanding.

Examining the text in advance of reading is another helpful tactic. Scan headers, subheadings, summaries, and any highlighted or bolded language to gain an overview of the content. As one reads, this initial scan facilitates the construction of a conceptual framework, which makes it simpler to incorporate additional information. The brain processes information more quickly and accurately when it has context for what it is about to encounter. Furthermore, previewing may assist in identifying essential passages that call for a slower, more concentrated reading pace, maximizing the trade-off between reading speed and understanding.

Active reading strategies are also essential for reading comprehension to be maintained at faster speeds. Asking questions, providing summaries, and making predictions about the material are all examples of active reading. Readers can stay focused and actively seek answers as they read by posing questions about the content. Reiterating text passage summaries in one's own words improves comprehension and memory. Anticipating the text's next move keeps the reader interested and focused, which is especially crucial while reading quickly. Even at faster rates, comprehension is improved by these strategies, which promote deeper processing of the content.

Using pacers or guides is another helpful tactic. A pacemaker—a finger, pen, or electronic device—can assist in smoothly guiding the eyes around the text and promote a steady reading speed. This technique aids in avoiding regressions, which are the propensity to go back and reread passages that can impede reading flow and decrease reading speed. Readers can train their eyes and brain to process information more quickly by reading at a constant speed. This may eventually cause reading speed to rise without reading comprehension falling off.

Another method that can significantly improve reading performance is chunking. Rather than reading words one after the other, this entails organizing words into meaningful units or sentences. The human brain can process Bits of information more efficiently than words. Readers can read more quickly without sacrificing understanding by practicing chunking. For example, the statement "The quick brown fox jumps over the lazy dog" might be recognized by the reader as three chunks rather than nine independent words: "The quick brown fox," "jumps over," and "the lazy dog." This enables quicker processing and lessens cognitive burden.

Maintaining a balance between speed and comprehension also requires increasing focus and concentration. Distractions are common in our digital environment, and staying focused can be difficult. Enhancing concentration can be achieved through practices like mindfulness and meditation. Furthermore, focusing can significantly increase by setting up a distraction-free reading atmosphere. Even at faster reading speeds, readers are more likely to retain comprehension when they are completely engrossed in the content.

Finding the ideal balance can also be aided by routinely practicing fast reading. Reading effectively requires practice, just like any other talent. To progressively raise their reading speed while keeping an eye on comprehension, readers can begin by setting incremental targets. Several apps and programs for speed reading offer workouts and feedback to help increase reading efficiency. Speed reading skills can be developed without losing comprehension via consistent practice and self-challenge.

Ultimately, it's critical to recognize that not all texts are appropriate for rapid reading. To properly understand the intricacies and details of complex or thick texts, such as academic papers, technical manuals, or literary classics, one must frequently read more slowly and deliberately. Under such circumstances, it is preferable to give comprehension precedence over speed. Understanding when to slow down and take extra time is essential to balance speed and comprehension.

Balancing reading speed and understanding is a dynamic, complex task that calls for various approaches. Practical strategies for sustaining comprehension at faster reading speeds include practicing chunking, sharpening attention, utilizing pacers, previewing text, utilizing active reading strategies, increasing vocabulary and prior knowledge, and engaging in frequent practice. People can improve their reading comprehension and efficiency by incorporating these strategies into their routines, making them more productive and involved readers. The ultimate objective is to read more effectively, with a more profound comprehension and improved memory of the content, rather than just faster.

CHAPTER III

Preparing for Speed Reading

Setting Realistic Goal

Realistic goal-setting is crucial for both professional and personal growth. Establishing quantifiable goals and individual objectives provides a clear path to success and helps you feel purposeful and directed. To guarantee that the goals stay relevant and reachable, this process entails analyzing one's aims, breaking them down into manageable milestones, and regularly assessing progress. People can improve their sense of overall success, productivity, and motivation by setting realistic goals.

Establishing personal goals is an essential first step in creating a goal. Individual objectives are the big, overarching goals that represent a person's beliefs, passions, and life goals in the long run. These goals can cover many topics, such as relationships, employment, education, health, and personal development. Engaging in self-reflection and introspection is crucial for adequately defining personal aspirations. Examining one's interests, advantages, disadvantages, and basic principles is part of this. People can create meaningful goals that align with their ambitions by clearly understanding what matters most.

The next step is defining personal objectives and breaking them down into measurable, specific targets. Quantifiable targets are actual accomplishments that act as standards for advancement. They give a precise picture of what must be accomplished and by when. To be effective, goals must meet the SMART criteria (Specific, Measurable, Achievable, Relevant, and Time-bound). Well-defined goals provide a clear picture of what has to be done, eliminating any possibility of confusion. Measurable targets enable individuals to objectively monitor their progress by giving tangible markers of accomplishment. Realistic and attainable goals consider each person's present resources and abilities. Relevant goals support the attainment of the larger personal goals and align with them. Time-bound objectives have set deadlines, which instill a sense of urgency and assist people in setting priorities for their work.

Achieving realistic goals requires balancing feasibility and ambition. Too-easy goals cannot motivate you enough, while too-ambitious goals can cause dissatisfaction and fatigue. Evaluating one's resources and existing circumstances is critical to setting reasonable goals. This entails assessing the time, expertise, resources, and support networks. People who are aware of these limitations can design goals that are both challenging and manageable. Thinking about possible roadblocks and making backup plans is also a good idea. This proactive strategy aids in keeping the momentum going even in the face of obstacles.

Making an action plan is crucial to establishing quantifiable goals. The precise actions required to meet the objectives are outlined in an action plan. It divides the objectives into more achievable tasks and gives each work a deadline. This systematic approach guarantees that people understand precisely what has to be done at each step and offers clarity and direction. An action plan also makes it easier to track progress because it allows people to mark off accomplishments and gauge their growth. It is imperative to conduct periodic reviews and updates of the action plan to account for any shifts in circumstances and maintain the relevance of the objectives.

Keeping track of accomplishments is essential to creating goals that work. Monitoring one's progress toward goals regularly promotes a sense of success and helps pinpoint areas for development. This can be accomplished in several ways, including keeping a journal, utilizing digital tools and applications, or asking peers or mentors for input. Recognizing little victories along the road might help people stay motivated and laser-focused on their long-term goals. On the other hand, if progress falls short of expectations, it's critical to examine the causes and make the required corrections. Setting, observing, and fine-tuning goals iteratively guarantees ongoing development and flexibility.

Including other people in the goal-setting process can offer necessary accountability and support in addition to personal commitment. Establishing a network of support and motivation among friends, family, and coworkers is facilitated by sharing goals. Additionally, it adds a layer of accountability because people are more likely to stick with their plans when they are aware that others are aware of them. Getting advice from mentors or coaches can also offer perceptions and methods for overcoming obstacles and maintaining focus.

Setting and achieving realistic goals has significant psychological advantages. Well-defined, quantifiable goals give a feeling of direction and purpose, which is crucial for mental health. Dopamine, a neurotransmitter linked to pleasure and reward, is released when goals are met, no matter how tiny. This pushes people to pursue more accomplishments and reinforces positive conduct. Additionally, pursuing goals fosters the growth of critical life skills like perseverance, problem-solving, and time management. These abilities are helpful in many facets of life and are transferable.

But it's crucial to recognize that goals are only sometimes reached in a straight line. There will be difficulties, failures, and periods of uncertainty. Maintaining your flexibility and being willing to change your goals when needed is critical. Once realistic goals may need to be adjusted as life circumstances change. This is not a sign of failure but instead of flexibility and staying true to one's changing priorities. Having a growth attitude and persevering through difficulties is essential for sustaining advancement.

To sum up, establishing reasonable goals is critical to professional and personal development. People can make a clear and organized route toward their goals by establishing quantifiable milestones and personal ambitions. Self-reflection, planning, progress tracking, and adaptability are all necessary steps. Setting and achieving realistic goals improves well-being, productivity, and motivation. They provide people with a feeling of purpose and direction, empowering them to succeed in significant and long-lasting ways. Good goal-planning concepts apply to all aspects of life, including job, education, health, and personal growth, and they promote a meaningful and purposeful journey.

Creating an Optimal Reading Environment

Improving concentration, understanding, and general enjoyment of reading depends on setting up an ideal reading space. To accomplish this, preparation—both mental and physical—is crucial. Reduced distractions and a comfortable environment allow readers to fully engage with the subject, creating a more satisfying and productive reading experience. This section discusses the significance of mental and physical preparation for setting up the best reading environment and provides tips for reducing distractions.

The first step in physical preparation is to choose a comfortable reading spot. Quiet, cozy, and interruption-free surroundings are great for reading. It is imperative to have a well-lit area because dim lighting can cause eye strain and weariness. If natural light isn't available, warm, gentle light from adjustable lights can still produce a calming atmosphere. Additionally crucial is cozy sitting. Having a chair that encourages proper posture while reading for extended periods can assist in avoiding physical discomfort. A neat and well-organized area can also lessen visual distractions and foster tranquility.

The selection of tools and reading materials can affect the reading environment and the physical arrangement. A dependable e-reader or high-quality print materials can improve the reading experience. Technical hiccups can be avoided when using digital gadgets by ensuring they are charged and have the latest upgrades. Accessory items like highlighters, bookmarks, and note-taking instruments should be easily accessible to encourage engaged and active reading of the content. Reading efficiency and enjoyment can be significantly increased by designing a physical space that suits each person's tastes.

Setting up an ideal reading environment also requires mental preparation. Deep reading and comprehension require a quiet, focused mind. Stress, anxiety, and task obsession can all be causes of mental diversion. Readers can resolve this by practicing mindfulness before and during reading sessions. Meditation, deep breathing techniques, or a quick stroll can all help reduce stress and enhance focus. A feeling of direction and purpose can also be obtained by clearly defining the reading session's intentions, including any desired results or objectives.

An essential component of mental preparation is time management. Setting aside specific blocks of time to read can aid in creating a routine and a mental space for the activity. This strategy improves focus and decreases the possibility of multitasking. Placing reading at the top of the list of essential and fun activities instead of as something to cram into a hectic schedule makes reading more enjoyable and engaging. People can psychologically prepare to connect deeply with their topic by prioritizing reading.

Reducing interruptions is essential to setting up the ideal space for reading. Distractions can come from internal and external sources, and dealing with them requires a diversified strategy. Noise, human interruptions, and computer notifications are examples of external distractions. Stress, inertia, and meandering thoughts are examples of internal distractions. By identifying and mitigating these distractions, readers can improve their comprehension and level of focus.

Controlling external distractions is frequently more straightforward. Establishing a peaceful area for reading is crucial. This could be setting up a quiet workspace, putting on noise-canceling headphones, or turning on calming background music that helps with focus. Minimizing interruptions can also be achieved by discussing the value of uninterrupted reading time with family members or roommates. Going to a quiet café or library can help create a more comfortable reading environment if you live in a noisy place.

One of the primary sources of outside distractions is digital gadgets. Computers, tablets, and smartphone notifications can seriously impede reading flow. Readers can lessen this by turning off notifications using settings like "Do Not Disturb" or "Airplane" mode. Devoted e-readers without internet connectivity can also reduce the desire to check social media or search the web. A concentrated reading atmosphere can be created by designating tech-free areas or periods.

A more contemplative approach is necessary for internal distractions. Stress or being preoccupied with other things might cause mental clutter, making it difficult to concentrate when reading. Focus can be increased, and mental clarity can be achieved by engaging in stress-reduction and mindfulness practices. Establishing attainable reading objectives can help focus and motivate the reader, which lessens the chance of daydreaming. Maintaining focus and avoiding mental tiredness can also be achieved by dividing reading sessions into manageable portions with brief pauses in between.

Active reading techniques can help improve focus and understanding even more. Asking questions, summarizing, and annotating the material are all part of active reading. This method lessens the chance of dozing off and keeps the mind active. Understanding and retention can be deepened by strategies including underlining important points, making notes, and talking with others about the content. By actively participating, readers can stay focused and comprehend the text at a high level.

Establishing a ritual for reading before bed is another helpful tactic for reducing distractions. This routine may involve creating clear objectives for the meeting, arranging the reading area, and preparing the required supplies. Maintaining a regular pre-reading routine facilitates the easier shift into a focused state by alerting the brain when it's time to focus. This practice can become a potent cue for the mind to shift into a focused, attentive reading state over time.

Creating the ideal setting for reading also involves maintaining physical health. A healthy diet, regular exercise, and enough sleep all support general cognitive performance and focus. Physical discomforts can be major distractions, such as hunger or exhaustion. Readers can ensure they are in the best possible shape to focus on their material by caring for their physical well-being.

In conclusion, preparing physically and mentally for reading and employing techniques to reduce distractions are all necessary to create the ideal reading environment. Readers can establish a physical atmosphere that facilitates comfort and focus by arranging necessary items, choosing an appropriate location, and creating a well-lit and cozy room. Mental preparation improves focus and engagement with the content. It includes time management, mindfulness practices, and intention setting. Reducing internal and external distractions with various techniques guarantees a more focused and productive reading experience. By prioritizing these factors, people can improve their reading comprehension, efficiency, and general enjoyment, making reading a more rewarding and engaging pastime.

Tools and Resources

The capacity to read rapidly and efficiently without losing comprehension is becoming increasingly important in our fast-paced environment. Various tools and resources, such as devices, applications, and books, can significantly aid the development and improvement of fast reading skills books. Technology can expedite the procedure and increase its effectiveness and accessibility for various readers. This section addresses how technology can be used to accomplish speed reading and looks at suggested books, apps, and gadgets that can help.

Foundational materials that offer insights into methods and approaches for enhancing reading comprehension and speed are books on speed reading. "Breakthrough Rapid Reading" by Peter Kump is one of the most well-known works on this topic. Kump's book provides a thorough plan for accelerating reading speed, complete with valuable drills and activities that will challenge the reader beyond their comfort zone. In addition, it offers knowledge retention techniques and stresses the value of consistent practice—both essential for proficient speed reading.

Tony Buzan's "The Speed Reading Book" is also highly recommended. Expert in mind mapping and mental literacy, Buzan offers strategies to increase reading speed two or three times without compromising understanding. His method blends cutting-edge mental organizing and retention tactics with tried-and-true speed reading approaches. Buzan's book benefits people who want to improve their reading comprehension and general cognitive ability more contemporary perspective; Howard Stephen Berg's "Super Reading Secrets" provides many techniques that significantly boost reading speed. Known for being the fastest reader in the world, Berg discusses methods he has refined over years of professional training and life experience. To read more quickly, his book offers helpful tips on how to get beyond common reading challenges, including regression and subvocalization.

Different applications have been created to help with the practice of speed reading in addition to books. The most downloaded app is called "Spreeder." With a technique known as Rapid Serial Visual Presentation (RSVP), words are displayed in the center of the screen one at a time in rapid succession by Spreeder. This method reduces the time spent on each word, training the brain to digest information more quickly. Moreover, users can modify the text's complexity and speed on Spreeder, making it appropriate for all reading levels.

Another useful app is called "Acceleread." Accelerated provides an individualized training program that adjusts based on the user's success, catering to novice and proficient readers. The software has activities to increase understanding, decrease subvocalization, and improve eye movement. Additionally, it monitors performance over time, giving users data and thorough feedback to measure their progress.

Another noteworthy app that uses RSVP technology is "ReadMe!" Users can import their reading materials because it supports various file types. ReadMe! is a flexible application for practicing speed reading because it allows you to customize the font size, backdrop color, and reading speed. Because the app syncs across many devices, users may practice their speed reading skills anywhere and anytime.

Dedicated speed reading devices can offer an even more engaging experience than apps. A portable scanner that scans text digitally and either reads it aloud or shows it on a screen is called the "IRISPen Air 7". This machine is beneficial for anyone needing to process printed books or documents quickly. The IRISPen Air 7 combines conventional reading materials with contemporary technology through text digitization, enabling users to employ fast reading software on PCs or mobile devices.

The "ReMarkable 2," a digital notepad with reading, writing, and annotation capabilities, is another cutting-edge gadget. The ReMarkable 2's e-ink display offers a paper-like reading experience, which might lessen eye strain during extended reading sessions even though it isn't designed as a speed reading aid. It is a valuable tool for organizing and maintaining reading materials because of its syncing capabilities with cloud services and integration with other digital applications.

Another device that can help with rapid reading is the "Kindle Oasis." Features like the ability to rapidly seek up definitions, change the background lighting, and vary the text size on Amazon's Kindle Oasis can all improve reading. Long-term comfort is ensured by the device's lightweight and ergonomic design, which also offers access to a wide variety of reading materials thanks to its enormous e-book collection.

Technology can help in fast reading in various ways, from specific tools and gadgets to entire systems and platforms. Platforms like Udemy and Coursera offer webinars and online courses with systematic training regimens for fast reading. These courses provide a comprehensive method for improving speed reading abilities and frequently include interactive exercises, video lectures, and community assistance. These might be especially helpful for students who like guided instruction with the opportunity to ask questions and get instructor responses.

Furthermore, browser extensions like "SwiftRead" have the power to change how people interact with digital content entirely. Previously called "Spreed," SwiftRead is an addon allowing rapid reading within web browsers. It's an excellent tool for professionals, students, and ardent readers who spend a lot of time online because it lets users quickly read web pages, PDFs, and other online documents. SwiftRead assists users in developing their speed-reading abilities practically and efficiently by incorporating speed-reading techniques into regular browsing activities.

In addition, research examines the possibilities of using augmented reality (AR) and virtual reality (VR) technology as speed reading aids. Users can practice and improve their speed reading skills in new ways by using

VR and AR to build immersive settings that imitate various reading contexts. These innovative tools, which provide incredibly interactive and engaging experiences, can potentially transform the way we teach reading thoroughly.

In conclusion, the growth and improvement of speed reading abilities can be significantly aided by various tools and resources, such as books, applications, and devices. Well-known publications with essential knowledge and strategies include "Breakthrough Rapid Reading," "The Speed Reading Book," and "Super Reading Secrets." Applications like "Spreeder," "Acceleread," and "ReadMe!" provide customized and interactive learning experiences. The "IRISPen Air 7," "ReMarkable 2," and "Kindle Oasis" are just a few examples of devices that combine technology and conventional reading methods to make reading more satisfying and productive. Browser extensions, online courses, and new VR and AR technologies further increase the options for training in rapid reading. People can improve their reading comprehension and speed with the help of these materials, which will make them more productive and engaged readers in today's fast-paced environment.

CHAPTER IV

Techniques for Speed Reading

The Basic Techniques

Compelling reading while retaining comprehension is a valuable ability, especially in this day and age where information overload is a frequent problem. Simple strategies like chunking words, skimming, and scanning can significantly increase reading efficacy and speed. Gaining knowledge of and proficiency with these methods can change how people interact with texts and enable them to precisely and swiftly extract relevant information. This section examines these core methods, explaining their significance, workings, and advantages.

Techniques

There are numerous speed-reading techniques that individuals can use to improve their reading speed and comprehension. Here are 10 specific techniques that can be effective:

A method for gaining an overview of the content is skimming. Understanding the basic ideas without becoming bogged down in the more minor details entails quickly scanning the text with the eyes. Skimming is very helpful when readers need to assess a document's significance, comprehend the primary organization of a text, or identify particular passages that demand more reading. Readers should concentrate on essential components when skimming content, including headings, subheadings, introduction paragraphs, and conclusions. Furthermore, a paragraph's opening and last phrases frequently include enough information to be understood about the subject. With this approach, readers can swiftly cover a lot of territory and choose which passages require more focus for a more in-depth reading.

On the other hand, scanning is a method for locating certain information within a text. In contrast to skimming, which aims to grasp the main idea, scanning entails searching for specific words, phrases, or information. This strategy is very effective for jobs like locating a date in a historical text, a definition in a technical manual, or a specific fact in a research paper. Readers can optimize their scanning by using visual cues like bold text, bullet points, or italics to help them find what they want. Maintaining focus and expediting the process can be achieved by rapidly moving the eyes down the page and following the lines with a finger or pointer. Although it takes practice to balance speed and accuracy, scanning is vital for rapidly extracting relevant information from large documents.

Chunking words are grouped and read as a single unit, improving reading comprehension and speed. This approach differs from the typical practice of reading word by word, which can be laborious and slow. When words are grouped to produce meaningful phrases or concepts, the human brain processes these groupings of words more quickly than individual words. For instance, a reader can comprehend a statement more quickly by chunking it into two sentences, "The quick brown fox" and "jumps over the lazy dog," rather than reading it as nine individual words. Chunking encourages readers to think in larger conceptual units rather than isolated words, which speeds up reading and helps with comprehension and retention.

Readers might begin practicing chunking by noticing the words and clauses that naturally split sentences. At first, it can be helpful to use visual aids like highlighting word groupings or drawing lines between chunks. As you practice, the eyes and brain will eventually become more adept at identifying and processing portions. Reading aloud in short bursts can help strengthen this strategy as well since it compels the reader to pronounce and see word clusters together. Readers will see a higher reading speed and a deeper understanding of the content as chunking becomes more automatic.

These methods work well together and can be combined to meet various reading objectives. They do not conflict with one another. To improve understanding and memory, a reader may, for example, skim a chapter to obtain an overview, scan it for keywords or specific information, and then chunk phrases during a thorough read. It takes awareness and adaptability to integrate various strategies, enabling readers to modify their strategy according to the content and goals.

Gaining proficiency in chunking, scanning, and skimming has many advantages. These methods help save time, which is very beneficial in professional and academic contexts where much reading is frequently necessary. Through expedited extraction of crucial information, they augment efficiency and production. Furthermore, by encouraging active interaction with the text, these strategies enhance understanding and retention. Readers participate in mental mapping when they skim or scan, arranging material to aid in recollection. On the other hand, chunking promotes more thorough information processing, which is essential for comprehension and long-term memory.

Teaching pupils these strategies in a classroom can significantly enhance their academic achievement and reading comprehension. Pupils proficient in chunking, scanning, and skimming are better able to manage extensive reading content, do well on tests, and interact critically with texts. As students get more proficient at organizing their reading assignments and gathering important information independently, these abilities also support independent learning.

These methods are also helpful in professional settings. Workers adept at swiftly scanning reports for pertinent information, chunking material for easier comprehension, and doing so are more productive and efficient in their jobs. These abilities can increase productivity, decision-making, and information overload management. Knowledge of these methods can give a substantial competitive advantage in domains where quick and accurate information processing is essential, such as research, media, and law.

Furthermore, in this day of widespread digital reading, similar methods can be modified with e-books, online articles, and PDFs. Digital resources such as software and tools can help in skill development. For example, apps for speed reading frequently include chunking, scanning, and skimming activities that allow users to practice these strategies under guidance.

To sum up, chunking, scanning, and skimming are fundamental strategies that can change how people approach reading. By learning these techniques, readers can become more proficient in their academic, professional, and personal lives, improving their speed, understanding, and recall. In a world where information is abundant and changing frequently, having the capacity to extract and process information quickly is crucial. By using and practicing these strategies, readers can read complicated texts more confidently and efficiently, improving their comprehension and interest in the subject matter.

Advanced Techniques

Reading well and thoroughly can be significantly improved using sophisticated strategies like meta-guiding, pointer techniques, and expanding peripheral vision. These methods enhance reading comprehension, speed, and focus by building on fundamental speed reading tactics. By learning these sophisticated techniques, readers can digest information more efficiently and become more adept at handling large amounts of material. This section examines the fundamental ideas and practical uses of pointer techniques, meta-guiding, and peripheral vision extension, emphasizing the advantages of each and offering helpful advice.

Meta-directing is a technique that involves guiding the eyes along the text lines using a finger, pen, or pointer. It is also referred to as hand pacing or guided reading. This technique lessens the propensity to regress or go backward while maintaining a steady reading rate. Readers can minimize distractions and improve focus by following the pointer by training their eyes to go smoothly and consistently over the page. For those new to speed reading, meta-guiding can be very helpful since it offers a concrete point of reference that helps them stay focused.

Readers should first choose a pointer that is comfortable for them to use, like a pen or their finger, before practicing meta-guiding. The pointer is moved consistently but slightly quicker than they usually read the text. The movement can be made slowly to give the eyes time to get used to tracking the pointer. However, with practice, the speed can be gradually increased. Encouraging the eyes to follow the pointer instead of skipping around the page increases the fluidity and speed of reading. Readers can experiment with different sorts of pointers and speed adjustments as they gain more experience to see what suits them best.

Though it focuses more on applying particular pointer types to improve reading efficiency, the pointer technique is closely related to meta guidance. For example, some courses on speed reading advise utilizing a digital program that mimics the movement of a pointer across the screen or a laser pointer. These technologies can provide more accurate control and visibility, particularly when reading on digital devices. The pointer method can be beneficial when reading thick or technical literature, where comprehension depends on keeping a constant pace and focus.

The pointer approach also includes modifications like underlining or circling words and phrases to highlight crucial information. This active interaction with the text facilitates better memory and comprehension of the content. Readers may swiftly recognize and remember important ideas by using the pointer to highlight important points, which makes reading more engaging and dynamic.

In addition to meta-directing and pointer approaches, peripheral vision extension is another sound, sophisticated technique. The ability to see and absorb information beyond one's direct line of sight is known as peripheral vision. By enabling readers to see longer passages of text at a glance, expanding their peripheral vision helps them read more quickly and effectively. This method lessens the need to focus on each word by teaching the eyes to recognize and analyze words and phrases outside of the center focus area.

Readers might begin by practicing exercises to expand their range of vision to practice peripheral vision expansion. One helpful practice is holding a book or screen at a suitable distance and attempting to read the text without moving your head or eyes. To read the words on each side of the core focus, readers should instead rely on their peripheral vision. This exercise can help the eyes absorb and process data from various sources over time.

Using applications or flashcards simultaneously displaying many words or lines of text is another way to increase peripheral vision. By rapidly skimming these cards or screens, readers may train their eyes to identify and understand the text without having to focus on every word. Through consistent practice, readers can improve their ability to scan longer passages of text at a glance, which will lead to a noticeable increase in reading speed.

A thorough system for advanced speed reading combines meta guidance, pointer techniques, and peripheral vision expansion. Readers can have a more effortless and productive reading experience by using a pointer to guide their gaze while increasing their peripheral vision. Faster information processing is made possible by this combination, as the pointer guides the eyes as they smoothly read the text, and the peripheral vision takes in and interprets surrounding words and phrases.

These sophisticated methods offer advantages that go beyond faster reading. Enhanced concentration and focus are two of the most significant benefits. Readers are less likely to become sidetracked or lose their position in the text when they use a pointer or guide. This prolonged focus improves understanding and recall because the mind can interact with the information without constantly being distracted. Furthermore, moving the eyes and widening the field of vision encourages interaction with the material, which fosters critical thinking and a deeper comprehension of it.

Additionally, applicable in many situations, advanced reading strategies have numerous uses. Students can tackle lengthy reading lists and challenging texts more skillfully in academic contexts if they can read more quickly and comprehend what they read. These abilities can improve efficiency and productivity in work settings, especially when examining technical materials, articles, or reports. Furthermore, advanced reading strategies can improve readers' particular reading experiences by making it easier and more enjoyable to appreciate literature and informational texts.

However, determination and practice are necessary to become proficient with these methods. By progressively incorporating meta-guiding, pointer techniques, and peripheral vision exercises into their daily reading routines, readers should approach the learning process with patience and persistence. Reading comprehension and speed can be significantly increased with consistent practice and a willingness to try new things and adapt.

To sum up, sophisticated strategies like meta-guiding, pointer approaches, and peripheral vision extension effectively improve reading comprehension and efficiency. While pointer approaches offer precision and connection with the text, meta-guiding offers an organized way to keep a steady reading pace. Thanks to expanding peripheral vision, readers can read faster by processing longer text passages at a glance. Through the integration of these strategies, readers can attain a reading experience that is more seamless, concentrated, and efficient. These abilities help people handle the large volumes of information encountered in daily life with better proficiency and confidence, making them useful in academic, professional, and personal contexts. Gaining proficiency in these advanced reading strategies can change how people engage with and understand written content if they put in the necessary effort.

Practical Exercises

Daily drills and real-world activities are necessary for developing fast reading skills. Targeted exercises can improve comprehension, reading speed, and general efficiency. This section provides step-by-step instructions to enable successful practice as it examines various real-world tasks to enhance speed reading abilities.

A fundamental practice for reading quickly is the "Pointer Method." This technique minimizes distractions and encourages a consistent reading pace by moving the pointer, pen, or finger across the text. The Pointer Method can be practiced by choosing a text and following each line from left to right with a pointer. As you get acquainted with the technique, start at a comfortable pace and progressively pick up the tempo. To minimize regression, concentrate on moving the pointer smoothly and without stopping, teaching your eyes to follow the movement.

"Chunking," a technique that involves reading words as a single unit after grouping them, is another helpful practice. This method lessens the number of discrete fixations your eyes make, which speeds up reading. Choose a paragraph and draw vertical lines between groups of three to five words to practice chunking. Read each group, not just the words that catch your attention. To help with the grouping, read aloud at first. However, as you get better, try reading silently. To improve your speed even further, gradually increase the quantity of words in each piece.

A digital exercise called "Rapid Serial Visual Presentation" (RSVP) shows words one at a time at a predetermined pace. This technique lessens the propensity to subvocalize and trains the brain to digest information fast. Use an app or internet resource that facilitates RSVP practice. As you get more comfortable, start at a low pace and progressively raise the words per minute. Instead of trying to pronounce the words, concentrate on understanding them as they come out. Frequent practice with RSVP can significantly improve your capacity to process information and read faster.

Exercises under "Peripheral Vision Expansion" are intended to increase your field of view so you can read more text simultaneously. In one task, you take a printed phrase and cover the middle with a card so that only the corners are visible. Using only your peripheral vision, try to read the visible words without bringing your gaze to them directly. The "Eye Span Drill" is an additional practice activity that involves reading longer text passages. Try reading two or three words simultaneously on either side of your main point of interest while choosing a paragraph. This practice improves reading speed by teaching your eyes to scan more words with each glance.

"Timed Reading" exercises let you track your development and establish goals for advancement. Choose a passage with a known word count to practice timed reading. Set a timer for one or two minutes and read as much as you can during that period. Once the timer sounds, count the words you read and determine your words per minute (WPM). Repeat this exercise frequently, trying to raise your WPM steadily without sacrificing comprehension. You will gradually increase your reading speed and self-assurance with this practice.

Exercises that include "skimming and scanning" are helpful for swiftly recognizing important information. Select a non-fiction article or textbook chapter to practice skimming. For a brief time—two or three minutes, for example—set a timer and attempt to summarize the key points without reading all the words. Pay attention to each paragraph's headings, subheadings, and opening and closing phrases. Set a specific search parameter for scanning, like a date, name, or term. Look swiftly over the text, focusing on the information you want. These activities help you become more adept at quickly identifying key features.

The "Preview and Review" strategy improves comprehension and memory by actively interacting with the content before and after reading. First, preview the text to practice this strategy. Examine the contents table, headings, subheadings, and any text that has been bolded or highlighted. This provides you with a summary of the main ideas and organization. Next, use your favorite speed reading strategies to scan the text. Once you're done, review the content by summarizing the key points in your own words. By doing so, knowledge is reinforced, and information is helped to stick in long-term memory.

"Mind Mapping" is an effective method for memorizing and organizing data. Find the main idea of a passage after reading it to practice mind mapping. Sketch the core node that symbolizes the critical idea on a blank paper. After that, make branches for details and subtopics and join them to the primary node. To convey ideas, use symbols, pictures, and keywords. This graphic representation improves memory recall and makes understanding the connections between concepts easier. Studying complex subjects and getting ready for tests are two areas where mind mapping comes in handy.

The "Backward Reading" exercise is a novel method that enhances focus and attention by upending established reading habits. To practice this exercise, choose a paragraph and read it backward, beginning with the final word and working your way to the first. This makes you focus on each word separately, sharpening your attention to detail and lessening the propensity to skip over words you know. Even though it's not a traditional reading technique, backward reading can improve comprehension and hone your general reading abilities.

Lastly, "Paced Breathing" techniques can assist with stress management and enhance reading focus. Sit comfortably and take a deep breath in for four counts, hold it for four counts, and then release it for four counts to practice timed breathing. Before you begin your reading session, repeat this breathing rhythm many times. This practice relaxes the body and mind, fostering a concentrated, at-ease condition ideal for reading.

In conclusion, it takes regular practice with a range of focused activities to build speed reading abilities. Comprehensive methods for improving reading comprehension and speed include the Pointer Method, Chunking, RSVP, Peripheral Vision Expansion, Timed Reading, Preview and Review, Mind Mapping, Backward Reading, and Paced Breathing. By gradually integrating these exercises into their daily routine, readers can enhance their abilities and become more proficient at managing extensive amounts of material. These methods can change how people read and process information, increasing their effectiveness and confidence as readers with commitment and consistent practice.

CHAPTER V

Building Speed Reading Skills

Developing Eye Movement Control

Gaining control over your eye movements is essential to increasing your reading comprehension and efficiency. Regression and backtracking are common problems that slow the reading speed and interfere with the learning flow. Effective eye coordination can lessen these problems. Readers can experience faster and more fluid reading by focusing on specific eye coordination exercises. This section addresses techniques to lessen regression and backtracking, explains the significance of eye movement control, and offers activities to enhance eye coordination.

Controlling eye movements is essential for reading. During reading, our eyes move quickly in a pattern known as saccades, alternating with brief stops known as fixations. The eyes take in and process the text during fixations. The goal of efficient reading is to maximize the information gathered during each pause while limiting the length and frequency of fixations. Poor eye movement control can be hampered by Reading comprehension and speed, typified by excessive fixations, regressions, and backtracking. As a result, mastering exact eye synchronization is crucial for proficient reading.

"Horizontal Line Tracking" is an essential exercise that helps with eye coordination. Through practice, the eyes will learn to glide over text lines without pausing needlessly. To complete this drill, draw multiple horizontal lines on a piece of paper, evenly spaced apart. Keeping your eyes steady and moving straight, start at the left end of a line and work your way gently to the right. For every line, repeat these steps, progressively quickening the pace as your eyes adjust to the movement. This practice lessens the need for repeated fixations by improving the capacity to read lines of text continuously.

One more helpful activity is "Peripheral Vision Training." Expanding their peripheral vision can increase reading speed and decrease the chance of regression by enabling readers to see more words at a glance. Choose a primary fixation point, like a letter or a dot on a page, to practice this. Recognize words or letters in your peripheral vision without shifting your eyes. Increase these peripheral items' separation from the core fixation point gradually. This practice helps your eyes learn to identify and process information outside your immediate field of vision, making reading more productive.

The "Zigzag Drill" is a dynamic workout that trains the eyes to follow non-linear routes, which enhances eye coordination. Draw a series of zigzag lines on a sheet of paper to practice this drill. Move swiftly and fluidly along the lines, starting at one end of the zigzag pattern and following it with your eyes. This exercise improves flexibility and coordination by testing the eyes' ability to adjust to sudden changes in direction. Readers who consistently practice the zigzag drill will better handle complicated text layouts and keep a consistent reading rate even when the text format changes.

Regression reduction—the ability to go back and reread passages of text—is essential for compelling reading. Poor eye coordination, inattention, or understanding issues are common causes of regressions. Regression can be reduced with ease using the "Finger Pacing" method. Readers can keep a steady reading pace and lessen the chance of becoming lost in the text by using a finger or pointer to guide their gaze along the lines. Additionally, by encouraging forward eye movement, this technique aids in maintaining the uninterrupted reading flow.

Furthermore, "Timed Reading" activities can lessen regression by enhancing focus and confidence. Choose a text piece to read aloud, then set a timer for a certain amount of time—for example, one or two minutes—to complete the activity. Aim to read as much of the passage as possible in the allocated time but at a comfortable pace. Once the timer has gone off, evaluate your understanding of the content. Timed reading exercises regularly encourage the eyes to move forward without stopping, lessening the tendency to return.

Enhancing understanding abilities is an additional tactic to reduce regression. Readers frequently regress because, on their first reading, they did not fully comprehend the content. Regression can be less necessary when using the "Previewing" strategy to improve comprehension. Before diving into a new text, spend a few minutes reading over the headings, subheadings, and any bolded or highlighted content. This summarizes the text's structure and content, making it more straightforward to follow and comprehend while reading it aloud. By establishing a mental framework, previewing lessens the possibility of misconceptions that result in regression.

One helpful strategy to improve eye movement control and decrease backtracking is to use the "Paced Reading" method. Paced reading establishes a steady reading rhythm with devices like digital applications or metronomes that offer visual or aural clues. Readers can maintain a consistent tempo and minimize eye movement disruptions by aligning their reading with these cues. Using this strategy reduces the likelihood of regression and backtracking since the eyes are trained to move rhythmically across the text.

Physical tools called "Reading Windows" or "Reading Strips" can direct eye movement and lessen distractions. A reading strip is a piece of paper or plastic with one or two lines of text visible at a time due to a thin window cut out. By advancing the strip down the page, readers can concentrate on the current line without being sidetracked by adjacent material. This gadget aids in preventing regression and promotes forward eye movement. Reading strips help improve eye coordination and encourage a more focused reading style.

Regression is sometimes caused by weariness; thus, incorporating "Eye Relaxation" activities into the reading regimen can also help and reduce eye coordination. The "20-20-20 Rule" is a proper relaxing technique that pauses every 20 minutes for 20 seconds to gaze at an object 20 feet away. This exercise eases the strain on the eye muscles and enhances the general health of the eyes. Readers can read longer and experience fewer regressions if they keep their eyes relaxed and synchronized.

Finally, developing long-lasting eye movement control requires incorporating these exercises and strategies into a consistent practice schedule. Maintaining consistency is essential; even a short daily practice session might result in noticeable gains over time. Starting with simple drills like tracking a horizontal line, readers should work up to more complex ones like zigzag patterns and training their peripheral vision. Readers can develop a fluid, productive reading style with less regression and backtracking through gradual eye strain and improved hand-eye coordination.

To sum up, mastering eye movement control is essential to raising reading comprehension and efficiency. While finger pacing, timed reading, and previewing aid in lessening regression and backtracking, exercises like horizontal line tracking, peripheral vision training, and zigzag drills improve eye coordination. These efforts can be strengthened by adding eye relaxation techniques and using tangible tools like reading strips. Readers can significantly enhance their reading comprehension and speed with regular practice and an organized method, resulting in more productive and pleasurable reading sessions.

Enhancing Vocabulary and Comprehension

Learning a language and developing literacy, vocabulary, and comprehension are fundamental building blocks. They are inextricably related, and a strong vocabulary is essential for understanding. Acquiring proficiency in these abilities is crucial not only for academic achievements but also for proficient communication in other domains of life. This section examines several methods for improving comprehension and expanding vocabulary, offering a thorough manual for teachers and students.

Building one's vocabulary is a dynamic process that goes beyond word memorizing. It entails awareness of the subtleties in word choice, usage, and context. Extensive reading is one helpful tactic. Learning new words in various situations is facilitated by reading various resources, including books, papers, and journals. This exposure aids in the natural comprehension of word meaning and usage. Furthermore, challenging reading materials can help readers learn and retain a new language by introducing it gradually.

One further important tactic is to keep vocabulary notebooks. Learners can methodically review and reinforce their vocabulary by meticulously recording new words, definitions, example sentences, and associated synonyms or antonyms in a customized notebook. This approach works exceptionally well when used in conjunction with many review sessions, giving the student opportunities to review and solidify their information.

Contextual learning is another effective strategy. Acquiring knowledge of words in the context of a sentence or narrative facilitates comprehension of the word's meaning and appropriate use. Techniques like cloze exercises, in which students use suitable vocabulary to fill in the blanks in a text, can help with this. These assignments help students think critically about word choice and context, improving their comprehension and memorizing new words.

Word association and mnemonics are beneficial for learning complex vocabulary. Students can establish mental associations that facilitate memory recall by linking unfamiliar words to well-known ideas, pictures, or noises. One may associate the word "gregarious," which means friendly, with the idea of a "gregarious" individual at a social event, for example. These mnemonic devices use cognitive psychology concepts to increase learning effectiveness and enjoyment.

Although having a large vocabulary is necessary for understanding, more is needed on its own. Comprehending a text entails knowing what words imply and appreciating its overall meaning, organization, and subtleties. In this context, active reading techniques are essential. This entails interacting with the material by posing queries, making predictions, clarifications, and summarizing. To sustain interest and enhance comprehension, readers might pose queries regarding the text and formulate guesses about its future events.

Summary is yet another important method. After reading, summarizing a passage's essential ideas aids with knowledge consolidation and comprehension of the text's central idea. Learners can practice expressing their information succinctly and clearly by practicing written summaries and oral recounts.

For those who learn best visually, graphic organizers like flowcharts, Venn diagrams, and mind maps are helpful.

These organizers aid in decomposing intricate information into digestible chunks, highlighting connections between various ideas, and offering a graphic synopsis of the book. For example, using a mind map to arrange a passage's key concepts and illustrative elements might help readers remember and comprehend the passage's general structure.

Inferencing is an essential reading comprehension skill. To do this, one must read between the lines to deduce conclusions, forecasts, and inferred meanings that must be made clear in the text. Exercises that require students to conclude the findings from provided data or forecast outcomes based on the context of the text help them practice inferencing. This improves the capacity for critical thought and deeper engagement with the content.

Collaboration and discussion are also crucial for improving understanding. Speaking with classmates or teachers about a text facilitates the sharing of various interpretations and points of view. This cooperative method can increase comprehension and provide fresh perspectives. Reading groups and literature circles are two examples of group activities that help students improve their understanding by allowing them to express their ideas, pose questions, and consider several points of view.

Although the techniques for improving comprehension and expanding vocabulary can be used alone, combining them can produce more successful learning outcomes. For example, while reading extensively, students can simultaneously concentrate on learning new vocabulary and practice comprehension techniques like inferencing and summarizing. This integrated method improves word knowledge and overall text comprehension by ensuring that vocabulary acquisition is contextually grounded.

Digital tools and technology can also be necessary in integrating these tactics. Engaging and effective vocabulary acquisition and comprehension practice can be achieved through interactive exercises, quizzes, and games available on educational applications and online platforms. Learners may quickly search for definitions and take notes with tools like built-in dictionaries and annotation features in e-books, which promote a seamless learning process.

In summary, improving vocabulary and understanding requires a diversified strategy incorporating several methods. Building a solid vocabulary requires a lot of reading, vocabulary notebooks, contextual learning, and mnemonics. Simultaneously, inferencing, graphic organizers, active reading, summary, and debate are essential for enhancing understanding. By combining these tactics, learners can gain a better comprehension and a more thorough command of the language. This all-encompassing strategy encourages academic success and gives students the tools they need for effective communication and lifetime learning.

Increasing Reading Speed Gradually

Swift and compelling reading is a priceless talent that improves academic achievement and personal growth. It takes time to increase reading speed while keeping comprehension and doing so involves organized practice, benchmarking, and regular progress monitoring. Furthermore, overcoming plateaus—times when progress appears to stop—requires persistence and focused tactics. This section examines the many methods for accelerating reading speed and emphasizes the value of benchmarks, progress monitoring, and plateau-busting techniques.

Individual differences in reading speed are mainly due to reading habits, cognitive processing speed, and subject matter knowledge. Setting a baseline is an essential first step in enhancing reading speed. This entails figuring out how quickly you read, usually expressed in words per minute (WPM). One may measure progress against an established reference point by creating a baseline. Additionally, it aids in establishing attainable goals that are appropriate for the individual's starting place.

Setting benchmarks is vital once a baseline has been established. Benchmarks are intermediate objectives that point the reader toward their ultimate speed goal. For example, intermediate benchmarks could be placed at 225, 250, and 275 wpm if the reader's baseline speed is 200 wpm and their objective is to attain 300 wpm. These incremental goals offer regular opportunities for motivation and evaluation while also helping to manage the overall aim.

Keeping track of your progress is essential to improving your reading speed. This entails scheduling consistent reading periods and keeping track of the words read and the amount of time spent. Readers regularly monitoring these indicators can spot patterns, acknowledge advancements, and adjust tactics. This process can be made more accessible with the help of various tools and apps that offer functions like speed tests, progress charts, and log readings. Keeping a thorough record helps spot trends and possible trouble spots and highlight accomplishments.

Readers frequently experience plateaus—times when their reading speed stays constant despite continuous effort— despite consistent practice and tracking. These plateaus must be broken through with focused tactics and an openness to change. A good strategy is to switch up the reading selection. Reading various books on different topics and genres helps improve one's general reading agility and cognitive flexibility. For example, changing from fiction to poetry or technical literature to fiction can stimulate the brain in new ways and possibly prevent stagnation.

Another tactic is to get better at comprehension. Inefficient understanding is often the cause of a reading speed plateau. Methods like scanning and skimming can be beneficial. While scanning seeks specific information or keywords, skimming entails quickly moving the eyes over the text to acquire the idea of the content. Using these strategies can improve their capacity for quick information processing, accelerating their reading speed overall.

Reading speed can also be significantly increased by reducing subvocalization, which is the practice of softly saying each word as you read. Subvocalization slows down speech but increases comprehension. Overcoming this hurdle may be aided by learning to visually recognize and comprehend words without pronouncing them. Subvocalization can be decreased with strategies like reading longer text passages at once and guiding your gaze with a finger or pointer.

Breaking through plateaus can also be facilitated through reading activities and consistent practice. The brain is trained to digest information faster through speed reading activities like rapid serial visual presentation (RSVP), in which words flash on a screen at progressively faster speeds. Regular practice of these activities can improve comprehension and quickness.

Furthermore, establishing clear, temporary goals might inspire the drive to break through plateaus. Practice sessions can gain concentration and intensity by imposing challenges, such as reading a certain number of words in a predetermined amount of time or finishing a book faster than usual. When these obstacles are overcome, one feels psychologically stronger and like they are progressing again.

Getting enough sleep and recovering from injuries is crucial for improving reading speed. The cognitive muscles in reading benefit from pauses, just as physical muscles do after strenuous activity. Burnout can be avoided, and high levels of motivation and mental performance can be maintained by getting enough sleep and partaking in relaxing and mind-refreshing activities.

It can be helpful to ask for assistance and feedback in addition to these tactics. Finding a reading partner or joining a group enables sharing strategies and experiences. Peer or mentor feedback can offer fresh perspectives and pointers for development. This cooperative method promotes community and mutual advancement and introduces novel tactics.

In the end, building reading speed gradually involves incorporating deliberate interventions, organized practice, and an emphasis on comprehension and speed. Establishing goals and monitoring advancements offer a clear path forward and encourage ongoing development. It takes adaptability, focused tactics, and a persistent mindset to break through plateaus. By adopting this comprehensive strategy, readers can improve their reading speed and experience in general, leading to new levels of productivity and satisfaction in their literary endeavors.

The path to faster reading is paved with purposeful repetition, regular assessment, and calculated tweaks. A baseline is established, and incremental benchmarks give direction and quantifiable objectives. Monitoring development regularly guarantees that advancements are identified, and tactics are modified as necessary. A combination of targeted workouts, better comprehension strategies, and various reading materials is needed to break through reading plateaus. Readers can improve their academic and personal lives by raising their reading speed gradually and successfully. This all-encompassing strategy guarantees that the procedure stays enjoyable, fruitful, and eventually satisfying.

CHAPTER VI

Speed Reading in Different Contexts

Academic Reading

Since it is the foundation for learning new information, carrying out research, and participating in scholarly discourse, academic reading is essential for both students and researchers. Strategic approaches to academic papers and textbooks and proficiency with note-taking and summarizing strategies are all necessary for compelling academic reading. This section explores academic reading habits and offers detailed advice on how to take and summarize notes efficiently.

When reading academic papers and textbooks, different techniques are needed than when reading for pleasure or general knowledge. Textbooks are frequently packed with material and organized to cover various subjects methodically. On the other hand, academic papers are typically divided into sections like introduction, methods, results, and discussion and present specific study findings. Efficient reading requires an understanding of the purpose and organization of these resources.

An overview is an excellent place to start while reading a textbook. A quick overview of the content can be obtained by skimming the table of contents, chapter headings, subheadings, and summary sections. This synopsis aids in identifying the primary ideas and subjects discussed, enabling readers to predict the text's substance and organization. Furthermore, reviewing any introductions or summaries can provide a brief grasp of each chapter's main ideas and goals.

An identical first step is helpful for academic writing. A summary of the study question, methods, conclusions, and overall significance of the work can be obtained by quickly reading the abstract, introduction, and conclusion sections first. This quick scan makes it easier to decide whether the document is worth reading in further depth and if it is relevant to the reader's area of interest.

For academic papers as well as textbooks, active reading is essential. This entails interacting with the text by asking, anticipating, and reflecting. Readers should think critically about the information as they read it, pose questions about what they learn, and consider how it connects to other information they may already know or have researched. This active participation improves understanding and helps the knowledge stick in your memory.

Taking notes well is an essential part of reading for academic purposes. Notes should concentrate on important ideas, arguments, and supporting data while capturing the spirit of the subject matter without becoming unduly technical. The Cornell Note-Taking System is one efficient way to take notes. The note page should be divided into three sections: a summary section at the bottom, a broader right-hand column for in-depth notes, and a narrow left-hand column for keywords and queries. This structure forces readers to break down the content into essential ideas and questions and combine them into a summary, promoting active involvement with the content.

Making use of mind maps is another helpful method. Mind maps are graphic representations of information where linked concepts radiate from the central idea, which is positioned in the center of the page. This approach works exceptionally well for arranging complicated data and finding connections between ideas. Readers can improve their comprehension and memory of the content by picturing it.

Another essential academic reading skill is summarizing. Condensing a text's significant concepts and important details into a brief form is summarizing. This procedure guarantees that the reader has understood the critical information and serves to reinforce understanding. Writing a brief synopsis summarizing the key points, research findings, and conclusions follows each section or chapter. This is a valuable method for summarizing information. This helps with understanding and offers a helpful reference for further review.

Concentrating on the research topic, methodology, findings, and conclusions is crucial while summarizing scholarly articles. A well-written summary should point out any limits or potential issues for more research and highlight the essential findings and their consequences. This brief synopsis might be helpful for research assignments or literature reviews.

The efficiency and efficacy of academic reading can be further increased by combining note-taking and summarizing strategies. For instance, after taking thorough notes on a textbook chapter or a scholarly work, readers can summarize their notes by condensing the most essential ideas. The content is guaranteed to be fully comprehended and kept thanks to this comprehensive approach.

Another essential component of academic reading is time management. With the amount of content researchers and students frequently have to cover, it's critical to manage time well and prioritize reading assignments. Establishing precise objectives, such as finishing a particular amount of chapters or papers in a predetermined time, can support motivation and attention. Furthermore, dividing reading assignments into smaller, more doable chunks helps reduce weariness and improve focus.

Adapting your reading methods to the content and goal is another intelligent tactic. For example, while intensive, active reading is best saved for in-depth study, skimming and scanning strategies can be employed for preliminary evaluations or when searching for specific information. With this adaptable method, readers can modify their strategies to fit the unique demands of each reading assignment.

Academic reading abilities can also be improved by interacting with mentors and peers. Getting teacher feedback or participating in study groups can yield fresh thoughts and viewpoints that enhance comprehension and promote critical thinking. Sharing strategies and ideas is another benefit of collaborative learning, which raises reading comprehension levels.

To sum up, proficient note-taking and summarizing abilities and strategic approaches to academic papers and textbooks are all necessary for compelling academic reading. Comprehension and retention can be significantly improved by beginning with an overview, actively reading, and using structured note-taking techniques like mind mapping or the Cornell system. Recapitulating strengthens comprehension and offers valuable references for later usage. Effective time management and adaptable reading strategies further optimize the reading process. Students and scholars can enhance their academic performance and scholarly endeavors by using these tactics to handle academic reading challenges successfully.

Professional Reading

Handling work-related documents like emails, reports, and memoranda in the workplace requires proficient reading skills. These documents are the foundation for business communications, transmitting updates, directives, and essential information. Creating reading strategies that can boost output, guarantee understanding, and support wise decision-making. This section examines professional reading strategies, emphasizing email, report, and memo management.

In the office, emails are a standard means of communication that frequently require quick attention and reaction. Effective reading techniques are crucial because of the sometimes overwhelming amount of emails received daily. Sorting emails according to significance and urgency is a helpful tactic. The reader can prioritize reading high-priority emails by using tools like email filters and flags to assist in categorizing communications. With this triage method, urgent or significant emails are dealt with right away, and less important ones can be looked over later.

Another essential email management strategy is systematic reading and replying to emails. It can be helpful to start by quickly scanning the inbox to find emails that must be responded to immediately. You can quickly determine the substance and urgency of any email by reading the subject line and the first few lines of the message. Emails that require a lengthy response or contain complex information might be flagged for later, more in-depth analysis. This preliminary scanning procedure keeps crucial emails from being missed and aids in efficient time management.

However, reports frequently include in-depth data and analysis, necessitating a more thorough reading strategy. Reading reports effectively requires attention to the essential parts and comprehending their format. Reports are usually divided into sections, with the executive summary, methodology, findings, and conclusions among them. The executive summary, which comes first, gives the reader a high-level overview of the report's key ideas and findings and makes it easy for them to rapidly understand the most essential details.

Skimming techniques can be used to find critical points and pertinent areas when reading the report's main body. Finding crucial information can be aided by paying close attention to headings, subheadings, and language that is bolded or highlighted. Graphs, charts, and tables are helpful focal points for compelling reading because they frequently summarize the data and findings concisely. Furthermore, a report's conclusions and recommendations section summarizes the most important findings and offers doable advice.

Taking notes when reading reports can be a constructive way to increase productivity. Concisely summarizing important information, supporting details, and conclusions makes it easier to remember and allow easy access later. Structured note-taking techniques, such as mind maps or the Cornell Note-Taking System, can help arrange information rationally and understandably. This exercise improves understanding and generates a valuable resource for decision-making and future reference.

Another popular method of communication in the workplace is the memo, which is usually used to deliver concise and targeted information. Reading memos effectively requires you to ascertain their main points and intent rapidly. Memos are typically brief and direct; therefore, it's critical to concentrate on the text's primary body. The main goal of the memo and any necessary activities can frequently be clearly understood by reading the opening and conclusion.

It is essential to use active reading tactics for all professional reading kinds. Questioning, summarizing, and reflecting on the material are integral to active reading. To assist in keeping attention and extracting relevant information, use questions such as "What is the main point?" and "What action is required?" Writing down the main ideas in your own words helps you remember and comprehend the material better. It also guarantees that the reading has value and can be used by having you consider how it will affect your decisions and activities.

Effective time management is essential to proficient professional reading. Setting aside particular periods to read memos, reports, and emails can help avoid interruption and manage workload. For example, you can keep emails from becoming a continual source of distraction by scheduling specific times during the day to read and reply to them. Comparably, setting up concentrated reading sessions for reports guarantees they get the time and attention they require without feeling hurried.

They are reducing distractions when reading is another helpful strategy. Enhancing comprehension and focus requires creating a noise- and interruption-free reading environment. Using devices like noise-canceling headphones and disabling notifications might aid in setting up a dedicated reading area. Long reading periods can also be avoided, and high levels of focus can be maintained by taking regular breaks.

Technology can help with professional reading as well. The reading process can be streamlined using digital tools, including note-taking applications, document readers, and email management software. Fast navigation and reference are made possible by features like annotation capabilities, highlighting, and keyword search. Additionally, digital platforms make it simple to organize and retrieve information, which improves productivity all around.

Ultimately, proficient communication abilities are essential for professional reading. Talking with coworkers about important documents can open up new ideas and points of view, improving comprehension and interpretation. Important reports and memos undergo collaborative review sessions to ensure crucial information is comprehended correctly and applied effectively. This cooperative method increases learning and promotes team cohesion and a common understanding.

To sum up, proficient reading of work-related documents like emails, reports, and memoranda is necessary for decision-making and successful communication in the workplace. Productivity can be significantly increased by setting priorities, handling emails in an organized manner, adopting structured reading techniques for reports, and paying close attention to the critical points in memos. Essential strategies for sustaining concentration and understanding include time management, taking thoughtful notes, and engaging in active reading. Technology use and encouraging teamwork in communication are further factors that promote compelling professional reading. By implementing these tactics, professionals can better manage their reading workload and maintain their knowledge, responsiveness, and productivity in their professions.

Leisure Reading

For many people, reading for pleasure is a treasured pastime that provides an escape into fantastical realms or a tour through the vast expanses of non-fiction knowledge. Speed reading strategies have become increasingly common as readers try to read more books in less time. When used carefully, these strategies can improve reading effectiveness without lowering reading enjoyment. The use of speed reading strategies for both fiction and non-fiction is examined in this section, along with tips for striking a balance between enjoyment and speed.

"Speed reading" refers to various methods to read text more quickly without appreciably compromising comprehension. Skimming, scanning, and limiting subvocalization are a few of these strategies. Applying these techniques to leisure reading is a problem because the main objective is frequent enjoyment and immersion rather than acquiring knowledge alone.

The story and the reader's emotional connection are critical components of fiction. To provide an immersive experience, fictional works frequently rely on character development, in-depth descriptions, and complex narratives. Fiction can be quickly read using speed reading techniques but proceed cautiously. Skimming is helpful, for example, while reading through slower passages or long details that add little to the story. Overusing skimming, however, could cause one to overlook the subtleties and emotional complexity of the narrative.

Changing the speed at which you read depending on the subject is one helpful strategy. One should read them carefully and slowly to truly understand the significance of crucial dialogue, pivotal plot points, and emotionally charged moments. On the other hand, less critical portions of the story, like repetitious or standard descriptions, can be read more rapidly. With this well-balanced method, readers can improve their reading efficiency and enjoy the novel.

To read fiction more quickly and enjoyably, try using your peripheral vision to read more words at a glance. Readers can read more soon by training their eyes to focus on word clusters rather than single words. While it takes skill and focus, this technique can significantly increase reading flow without compromising comprehension.

Contrarily, reading non-fiction frequently entails discussing concepts, arguments, and facts. Here, speed reading strategies can be beneficial because they allow readers to quickly sort through vast amounts of information. Scanning and skimming make critical information, primary ideas, and arguments easier. Generally, non-fiction writings are organized using headings, subheadings, and bullet points to make these strategies more straightforward by emphasizing key areas.

A specific goal is crucial when using speed reading for non-fiction. Whether the reader is trying to grasp a concept, find specific information, or assess an argument, they should know their objectives. This concentration aids in identifying the areas that can be skimmed and those that need to be read in full. For example, in a scientific report, the methodology and technical data can be skimmed unless directly relevant to the reader's objective. Usually, however, the abstract, introduction, and conclusion are adequate to understand the main findings and consequences.

Readers can use tools like highlighters and marginal notes to balance reading speed and understanding when reading non-fiction. To help with retention and speed up evaluations, highlight crucial points and make minor remarks in the margins. This method ensures that important details are noticed in the haste to finish reading.

Reducing the time spent silently pronouncing words as you read is another way to increase speed without sacrificing comprehension. This approach works exceptionally well for fiction as well as non-fiction. Readers can comprehend text more quickly if they recognize words and phrases as visual patterns instead of sounds. Reading speed can be gradually increased by using this strategy on more straightforward texts and then moving on to more complicated ones.

Even though speed reading has benefits, it's important to remember that leisure reading is mostly about enrichment and enjoyment. Reading is a very intimate and personal activity that offers many people emotional fulfillment, inspiration, and relaxation. As a result, finding a balance between reading rapidly and thoroughly appreciating the text is crucial.

To attain this equilibrium, you can allocate particular reading periods for various kinds. For example, when reading non-fiction for work or personal growth, fast reading methods can be used to acquire information during times set aside for learning. On the other hand, reading for pleasure can be done at a slower speed, which enables readers to get lost in the story and appreciate the storytelling.

Moreover, taking pauses throughout reading sessions can improve reading satisfaction and speed. Reading becomes less taxing and more pleasurable when interspersed with short pauses that prevent weariness and preserve concentration. This method helps the brain comprehend and integrate information more efficiently, especially when reading complex non-fiction texts.

Technology integration can also help strike a balance between fun and quickness. Fast reading features like movable font sizes, programmable margins, and even speed reading software that flashes words or phrases quickly are frequently included in e-readers and reading apps. These resources offer a flexible and customized reading experience by being able to be customized to individual tastes and reading objectives.

Knowing one's reading tastes and objectives is crucial to adapting speed reading strategies to leisure reading. Every reader reads at a different speed and in a way that best suits their comprehension and enjoyment. Through trial and error with various methods and tweaking them according to the genre and individual preferences, readers can strike a pleasing balance that improves their reading experience.

Finally, fast reading strategies provide valuable resources for improving reading effectiveness for both fiction and non-fiction. When used carefully, these strategies can improve time management and information processing for readers without compromising the pleasure and immersion of leisure reading. Various tactics, like changing the speed at which you read, reducing the amount of time you spend subvocalizing, and using tools like marginal notes and highlighting, might help you strike a balance between speed and enjoyment. Readers can increase their reading efficiency and enjoyment by understanding the differences between the demands of fiction and non-fiction and adjusting their reading strategies accordingly.

CHAPTER VII

Boosting Learning Efficiency

Cognitive Techniques for Better Retention

In today's information-rich environment, information retention and recall capacity are essential for success in the workplace, school, and personal life. Cognitive approaches like mnemonics and memory procedures can significantly improve comprehension and retention when paired with active reading strategies. This section examines several cognitive ways to improve recall, particularly emphasizing mnemonic devices, memory techniques, and successful active reading tactics.

The key to increasing retention is mastering memory skills. The loci approach, sometimes called the memory palace, is one essential strategy. Using this age-old tactic, one visualizes a place they are familiar with and associates specific areas with it. People can remember the information better if they mentally navigate the scene. For instance, seeing each item on a grocery list in a different house room can help you remember it. This technique uses spatial memory, which is frequently more durable and dependable than rote learning.

Chunking is an additional helpful memory trick. This entails dividing complex information into smaller, more digestible segments. For example, breaking up a large string of numbers, like a phone number, into manageable chunks makes it easier to recall (123-456-7890, for example). Chunking lessens the cognitive load and improves information structure, aiding the brain's ability to process and store information more effectively.

Mnemonics are an effective tool for helping people remember things. Mnemonics are devices that change the presentation of information to make it easier to recall. Acronyms are a frequent mnemonic device in which a new, easily remembered word is created using the initial letters of a succession of words. The Great Lakes, for instance, are easier to recall when you use the acronym HOMES (Huron, Ontario, Michigan, Erie, Superior). A further kind of mnemonic is the acrostic, in which a list's initial letters are combined to create a catchy phrase or statement. For instance, "Every Good Boy Does Fine" aids in helping music students retain the E, G, B, D, and F lines of the treble clef staff.

Songs and rhymes work well as mnemonics as well. Information can be retained longer when it has a song's melody and rhythm. For instance, many individuals can recall the alphabet because of the "Alphabet Song." Similarly, making a rhyme or melody to help remember challenging ideas or lists can significantly improve retention. These mnemonic devices function by activating different brain regions, which strengthens the encoding of the information.

Effective practices for active reading are equally crucial for improved comprehension and memory. Active reading calls for interaction with the text through summarizing, reflecting, and asking questions. This is in contrast to passive reading, which entails reading the text. SQ3R, or Survey, Question, Read, Recite, and Review, is a proper active reading technique. This approach encourages readers to scan the text at first by using headers, subheadings, and summaries to gain a quick overview of the text's substance. They then start to ask questions about what they hope to learn. They look for answers to these questions during the reading phase. After that, they evaluate the content to ensure knowledge and retention and repeat important passages from memory.

Annotating the text is an additional active reading technique. This includes writing marginal notes, emphasizing or underlining essential points, and summarizing parts using one's own words. In addition to keeping the reader interested, annotations produce a visual map of significant information that may be reviewed later. Actively noting and summarizing information facilitates information retrieval and helps to strengthen memory.

A visual active reading technique that improves recall is mind mapping. A mind map is a diagram that uses words, symbols, images, and lines to branch out from a central notion into related ideas. Complex concepts can be understood and retained more easily by mimicking the brain's natural information organization process. By making mind maps, readers can better understand concepts and the connections between disparate information pieces, improving recall and comprehension.

Moreover, imparting knowledge to others is a highly successful active reading technique. Giving explanations of concepts to others necessitates a thorough comprehension of the subject matter and supports one's learning. This approach, also known as the Feynman Technique, entails dissecting complex concepts into manageable chunks and imparting knowledge to oneself or another person. This procedure not only assesses comprehension but also identifies areas that require more study.

Another cognitive strategy that significantly improves recall is spaced repetition. Spaced repetition is going over material at progressively longer intervals throughout time, as opposed to cramming it all in one sitting. This method uses the psychological spacing effect, which postulates that learning something a few times over an extended period is easier on the memory than knowing a lot in a short time. Schedule reviews using tools like spaced repetition software or flashcards to ensure that knowledge transfers from short-term to long-term memory.

Retrieval exercise is a highly effective way to improve retention. This entails actively retrieving data without consulting the source. Effective methods for practicing retrieval include self-testing and employing flashcards. Neural pathways are reinforced when the brain is forced to retrieve information, facilitating future recollection of the knowledge.

Enhancing retention through multimodal learning is another benefit. Using all of your senses—auditory, visual, and kinesthetic—can aid with memory reinforcement. For instance, taking notes by hand stimulates the kinesthetic sense, but reading aloud stimulates the visual and auditory senses. More muscular memory development occurs when more senses are used during learning.

To sum up, cognitive strategies for improved retention include a variety of memory tactics, mnemonic devices, and active reading approaches. Memory strategies like chunking, spaced repetition, and the locus of attention method facilitate effective information organization and encoding. Mnemonic devices, such as rhymes, songs, acrostics, and acronyms, convert information into forms that are easier for people to remember. Active reading techniques that improve comprehension and retention include mind mapping, SQ3R, annotating, and the Feynman Technique. These techniques force readers to interact closely with the text. People can significantly increase their capacity to remember and retain information by incorporating these cognitive strategies into their study habits. This will increase their chances of academic, professional, and personal success.

Integrating Speed Reading with Other Learning Methods

Speed reading has become a valuable strategy for effective and efficient learning since it allows one to process and understand vast amounts of text rapidly. However, more than rapid reading might be for in-depth comprehension and long-term retention required. The synergistic effect of speed reading combined with other learning strategies like mind mapping, the SQ3R approach, and several multimodal techniques can improve learning outcomes. This section investigates how the synergy of multimodal learning might maximize learning by integrating fast reading with these approaches.

Techniques for speed reading entail increasing reading speed without significantly sacrificing understanding. These methods include reducing the amount of subvocalization, improving peripheral vision, and guiding the eyes using pointers. The main advantage of speed reading is the capacity to quickly skim through materials and discover key points and vital information in a fraction of the time it typically takes. While speed reading helps organize vast volumes of reading, it can be even more effective when paired with other techniques that improve retention and understanding.

Mind mapping is one such complementary technique. Using an essential notion at the center and related concepts branching out, mind mapping is a visual tool for hierarchically organizing data. The natural way the brain processes information is well-aligned with this technique, which facilitates comprehension and retention of complex subjects. Mind mapping can be used with speed reading to assist in swiftly extracting and visualizing the main concepts from a text. For example, after quickly reading a textbook chapter, making a mind map can help summarize the key ideas and how they relate to one another, giving a concise and well-organized summary. With its ability to simplify review and reinforce memory, this visual tool contributes to a more comprehensive learning process.

Another powerful learning technique that works well with fast reading is the SQ3R approach (Survey, Question, Read, Recite, and Review). By encouraging active involvement with the text, the SQ3R technique improves understanding and memory. Combining this strategy with rapid reading is one way to optimize efficiency. To provide the reader with an overview of the content, the Survey stage can initially be completed quickly, with the reader skimming headings, subheadings, and summaries. The reader creates questions regarding the text during the "Question" phase, establishing clear objectives for the reading session. During the Read step, one might utilize speed reading strategies to swiftly scan the material while concentrating on locating responses to the pre-formulated questions. The knowledge can then be reinforced by reciting and reviewing the content, and fast reading makes it possible to do several brief reviews to reaffirm what has been learned.

Learning can be significantly improved by multimodal learning, which incorporates using a variety of senses and learning modalities. Combining auditory and kinesthetic learning approaches with speed reading allows for flexibility in learning styles and strengthens comprehension. For instance, a peer discussion or explanation session after scanning a text can activate auditory learning pathways. Further cementing the knowledge in memory is kinesthetic learning, which can be triggered by summarizing or drawing diagrams. This multimodal approach improves information retention by ensuring that learning is thorough and tailored to each learner's strengths.

Combining digital tools with fast reading is another example of how multimodal learning works well together. Text-to-speech capabilities, interactive annotations, and font sizes that may be adjusted are just a few of the elements digital platforms frequently offer to encourage quick reading. These resources can help promote deeper learning and improve the reading experience. Text-to-speech, for example, can be used with speed reading to enhance comprehension by providing students with an aural way to reinforce what they read while they follow along in the text. Readers can rapidly add notes and highlight crucial topics with interactive comments, resulting in a personalized learning resource that can be reviewed effectively.

Effective cognitive load management is one of the main advantages of integrating fast reading with other learning strategies. The amount of mental work needed to process information is called cognitive load. By cutting down on reading time, speed reading frees up cognitive resources for in-depth comprehension and synthesis of the content. By organizing and structuring knowledge, mind mapping and the SQ3R technique lessen cognitive overload and facilitate understanding of complicated subjects. This harmony between taking in information quickly and digesting it systematically improves learning depth and efficiency.

Additionally, the combination of multimodal learning creates a more dynamic and captivating learning environment. Traditional reading can occasionally become boring and cause disengagement when reading anything dense and intricate. Combining several approaches keeps learning engaging and dynamic. One way to establish a dynamic learning environment and keep students interested and motivated is to alternate between mind mapping, fast reading, and peer discussions. This dynamic method increases memory and adds enjoyment and fulfillment to the learning process.

Multimodal learning also has the benefit of adapting to various demands and settings. Different approaches may be needed for other subjects and types of material. For instance, speed reading can be beneficial for swiftly going over literature and research papers, and it can be helpful to combine speed reading with mind mapping and the SQ3R approach for in-depth analysis of scientific books. This adaptability enables students to customize their approaches to the particular requirements of their learning goals, making the most of their study time.

In summary, combining the SQ3R method, mind mapping, and multimodal approaches with speed reading can produce a potent synergy that improves learning efficacy and efficiency. Speed reading makes it easier to absorb knowledge quickly, but techniques like mind mapping and SQ3R give learning structure and depth. Multiple senses and learning styles are engaged in multimodal learning, which improves knowledge retention and heightens the learning process. By combining these strategies, students may successfully regulate their cognitive load, adjust to various situations, and develop a balanced plan that optimizes their speed and comprehension. Multimodal learning's synergy ensures students can navigate the vast knowledge landscape with agility and depth. It is a holistic approach to education.

Continuous Improvement and Lifelong Learning

The quest for continual learning and constant improvement has become crucial for professional and personal progress in an ever-changing world. This journey revolves around the idea of a growth mindset, which highlights the conviction that improvement and development are possible via work and education. Furthermore, it's essential to keep up with new findings and methods to adjust to evolving possibilities and obstacles. To promote continual progress and lifetime learning, this section examines the significance of embracing a growth mindset and tactics for staying current with new findings and methodologies.

A growth mindset, coined by psychologist Carol Dweck, is the conviction that aptitude and intelligence can be enhanced by commitment, diligence, and endurance. This is in contrast to a fixed mindset, which holds that a person's intelligence and skill set are fixed characteristics that cannot be much altered. The cornerstone of continuous development is a growth mindset, which motivates people to take on obstacles, persevere in the face of failure, and view effort as a means of reaching mastery. People's perceptions of their talents are altered, from dreading failing to seeing setbacks as chances for improvement and education.

Developing resilience is one of the main advantages of a growth mindset. People are more inclined to take on challenges and persevere through hardships when they think they can improve their abilities. Resiliency is essential for lifelong learning because it helps people overcome the inevitable setbacks and disappointments that accompany trying new things. Those with a development mentality examine their errors, draw lessons from them, and keep improving rather than letting setbacks stop them. As students continue to learn and grow, this strategy eventually yields higher accomplishments.

A growth mentality also encourages curiosity and a love of education. Adopting this approach makes a person more receptive to new experiences and constantly looking to learn more. Instead of focusing solely on the results, they are driven by the learning process. This internal motivation, which propels people to seek new information and abilities throughout their lives regardless of rewards or acknowledgment from others, is essential for lifelong learning.

An additional essential component of lifetime learning, and continuous improvement is staying current with new findings and methods. The world of today moves quickly, and both information and technologies are constantly changing and keeping up with the most recent advancements guarantees that people can use the most recent and efficient techniques and stay relevant in their areas. A variety of methods can be used to accomplish this constant learning.

Taking advantage of professional development opportunities is one successful tactic. Attending conferences, workshops, and seminars lets people stay current on the newest technologies and trends, acquire fresh insights, and learn from peers and professionals. These gatherings also offer beneficial networking chances, allowing people to contact experts in related fields and share information.

Apart from official professional development, self-directed learning is an effective means of staying current with new findings and methods. Reading books, papers, and scholarly publications in one's area of interest might be part of this. Learn new skills and get new knowledge in a flexible and accessible way with online courses and webinars. Individuals can learn at their own pace and schedule by accessing various courses on Coursera, edX, and LinkedIn Learning.

Being a part of communities and professional groups is another crucial component of remaining current. Access to unique resources like online forums, research papers, and industry publications is frequently granted to members of these organizations. By getting involved in these groups, people can converse with others who share their interests and areas of expertise, pose questions, and share knowledge. This cooperative learning style encourages an ongoing flow of ideas and keeps people updated on the most recent advancements in their profession.

Utilizing technology is also essential for staying current with emerging fields of study and methods. You may follow industry professionals, academic institutions, and thought leaders using tools like social networking platforms, email newsletters, and RSS feeds. Thanks to these technologies, which offer a constant flow of information and updates, it is simpler to stay updated on the newest findings and trends. Additional resources like podcasts and YouTube channels provide professional opinions and conversations on various subjects, making learning while driving or doing other everyday tasks easy.

Another essential element of lifetime learning and ongoing growth is reflective practice. This entails routinely evaluating one's experiences, deeds, and educational procedures to pinpoint areas needing development and establish future objectives. Maintaining a learning journal can be valuable for recording reflections, monitoring development, and planning for future expansion. People can modify their learning approaches and professional practices by methodically examining the successful aspects and areas for improvement.

Continuous improvement can also be significantly aided by mentoring and coaching. Mentors and coaches offer direction, encouragement, and constructive criticism to help people overcome obstacles and realize their objectives. They can provide insightful viewpoints drawn from their personal experiences and areas of expertise, enabling mentees to uncover growth opportunities they might not have otherwise noticed. Developing a rapport with mentors and asking for their guidance helps hasten learning and growth.

And last, encouraging a culture of learning within companies can significantly help ongoing development.

Organizations that place a high priority on learning and development foster a culture where workers are motivated and assisted in pursuing personal growth. This can be accomplished by making training programs accessible, promoting teamwork and exchanging knowledge, and praising and rewarding efforts to grow and learn. Individuals gain from a learning-oriented culture, improving organizational performance and flexibility.

A growth mindset and remaining current with new findings and methods are critical components of lifelong learning and continual progress. People with a growth mindset can accept challenges and keep going after obstacles because it cultivates resilience, curiosity, and a love of learning. People stay relevant and productive in their areas by staying updated with new advancements through self-directed learning, professional development, professional community participation, and technology utilization. Supporting a culture of learning, mentoring, and reflective practice all contribute to ongoing development. Through the integration of various approaches, people can consistently improve their knowledge and abilities, leading to both personal and professional success in a constantly changing world.

CHAPTER VIII

Overcoming Challenges in Speed Reading

Common Obstacles and How to Overcome Them

Although reading is essential for education and personal growth, it can present its unique set of difficulties. Managing eye strain and weariness and navigating complicated texts and new subjects are some of the most frequent challenges. Tactical approaches and workable solutions are needed to overcome these obstacles and preserve general well-being while improving reading efficiency.

Readers need help with complex materials, be they literary works, technical documents, or academic papers. These publications frequently have complex reasoning, specialist jargon, and difficult-to-understand concepts. Use active reading techniques to tackle complicated books efficiently. Asking questions, summarizing, and annotating the text are all ways that active readers interact with the text. It is beneficial to quickly scan the text for the essential elements by glancing through the headings, subheadings, and summaries before delving into the content. This initial assessment helps create a reading goal and acts as a mental road map.

Completing complex literature into smaller, more digestible chunks can make them less intimidating. Readers can better absorb and comprehend the material by focusing on one section at a time and breaking the text into smaller chunks. Understanding and recall are strengthened by summarizing each portion in one's own words. Crucial information can also be identified and remembered with the help of annotations, which include underlining critical points, making marginal notes, and highlighting significant portions.

A typical first obstacle while learning about new subjects is a need for prior information. Readers might begin by looking up relevant introductory texts to lay this basis. These could be general articles, overview-focused films, or textbooks. Before reading more complicated materials, familiarizing yourself with the language and fundamental ideas can significantly enhance comprehension. Using glossaries and reference books can be helpful when searching for new terminology and concepts rapidly.

Using supplemental materials like podcasts, discussion boards, and lectures might help you learn more about subjects you need to learn more about. These resources offer a more thorough understanding of the subject matter by presenting information in various formats and viewpoints. Conferring with colleagues or subject matter experts can also dispel misconceptions and enhance knowledge. Engaging in study groups or topic-specific online communities can promote cooperative learning and reduce the fear of taking on new subjects.

Another typical issue with prolonged reading is managing eye strain and weariness. Extended reading sessions can cause discomfort and reduce reading effectiveness, mainly on digital devices. It is imperative to adhere to the 20-20-20 rule, which states that you should gaze at anything 20 feet away for 20 seconds every 20 minutes to reduce eye strain. This easy technique lessens tension and helps to relax the eye muscles. Eye strain can also be reduced by setting the screen's brightness and contrast to comfortable settings and ensuring the reading area is well-lit.

You are managing physical weariness while ergonomics greatly aids reading. Neck and back pain can be avoided by keeping proper posture, choosing a comfortable chair, and setting the reading material at the right height. It's crucial to take regular pauses to stand, stretch, and move around to keep your body relaxed and your mind sharp. Incorporating mindfulness and deep breathing exercises can help revitalize the body and mind during breaks.

Mental tiredness management is just as important as physical measures to maintain understanding and focus. Reading dense information or studying for extended periods without breaks can frequently lead to cognitive weariness. Readers can counter this by using strategies like the Pomodoro Technique, which calls for working for 25 minutes and then taking a 5-minute break. This approach promotes prolonged concentration while offering regular breaks for mental relaxation. Extended pauses, lasting roughly two hours, following every four cycles, can improve output even further and ward off fatigue.

Energy levels and cognitive performance are also impacted by nutrition and hydration. Sustained mental performance can be supported by eating a balanced diet high in fruits, vegetables, and whole grains and drinking lots of water. While it can be helpful in moderation, caffeine should be carefully consumed to prevent dependence and the ensuing energy collapse.

Creating a comfortable reading space is another essential element in conquering these typical challenges. A peaceful, well-lit, distraction-free environment fosters improved concentration and less eye strain. You can increase focus and reduce background noise by using noise-canceling headphones or relaxing background music. Keeping essential resources close at hand and organizing reading materials can also maximize reading efficiency and reduce disruptions.

Effective time management is essential to prevent fatigue and balance reading with other obligations. Having clear objectives and designating certain time blocks for reading can aid in efficient workload management. The process can be made more manageable and less daunting by setting priorities for your work and dividing more significant reading assignments into smaller, more manageable pieces. Maintaining organization and focus can be facilitated using tools like calendars, time-tracking applications, and to-do lists.

Overcoming reading hurdles also depends on motivation and thinking. It can make a big difference to approach complex texts and new subjects with a growth mindset and an optimistic outlook. Resilience and tenacity are fostered when obstacles are seen as chances for development and learning. Maintaining motivation and boosting confidence can be accomplished by establishing reasonable expectations and acknowledging minor victories.

To sum up, challenges related to reading comprehension include handling intricate texts and novel subjects and coping with eye strain and exhaustion. It will take a mix of tactical fixes and strategic thinking to overcome these obstacles. Active reading techniques that improve comprehension and recall of complicated materials include summarizing, annotating, and previewing. Gaining prior knowledge, using additional resources, and interacting with peers make it easier to comprehend new subjects. Maintaining a comfortable reading environment, taking frequent breaks, and adhering to ergonomic principles are all critical in managing eye strain. Maintaining motivation and focus over time is facilitated by addressing mental exhaustion through time management, healthy eating, and a positive outlook. By integrating these tactics, readers can improve their reading comprehension, efficiency, and overall experience, facilitating ongoing learning and personal development.

Staying Motivated

Motivation is the engine that propels success, achievement, and personal development. One must be motivated to be focused and dedicated to one's goals, whether seeking academic brilliance, career goals, or personal desires. This section examines practical methods for maintaining motivation, such as creating short- and long-term objectives and acknowledging progress.

The secret to maintaining motivation is to set attainable goals. Setting and achieving goals gives people focus, direction, and a feeling of purpose as they lead them toward their intended results. Short-term objectives are benchmarks that can be met quickly, including finishing a project phase, finishing a book chapter, or becoming an expert in a particular ability. These objectives give people concrete targets and a sense of accomplishment, which increases motivation as people witness the fruits of their labor.

On the other hand, long-term objectives cover more expansive ambitions that call for consistent work and devotion over a longer time frame. A few examples are a degree, professional advancement, business startup, or personal goals like learning a new language or finishing a marathon. Long-term objectives give people a sense of direction and purpose that extends beyond their current responsibilities, inspiring them to stick with it and overcome obstacles and disappointments.

Setting SMART goals—specific, measurable, achievable, relevant, and time-bound—is crucial to their success. Measurable goals offer a mechanism to monitor progress and assess achievement, whereas specific goals define precisely what must be done. Realistic and doable objectives take into account available resources and limitations. To ensure meaningful pursuit, goals should be relevant and in line with one's values, interests, and long-term aspirations. Last but not least, time-bound objectives include a deadline or timeline, which fosters accountability and urgency.

Long-term objectives can be made less intimidating and more achievable by breaking them down into minor, more doable activities. This method, chunking or job deconstruction, enables people to concentrate on one step at a time, sustaining their enthusiasm and forward momentum. Every accomplished job contributes to the overall goal, enhancing the sensation of accomplishment and providing the drive to keep going.

Honoring successes and turning them into milestones is a great way to keep momentum and drive. Acknowledging any progress, no matter how tiny, boosts confidence and encourages positive behavior. There are many different ways to celebrate, such as treating oneself to a modest treat, taking a moment to unwind and rejuvenate, or telling friends and family about achievements. These epiphanies not only provide you with a sense of accomplishment but also provide you with the drive to keep working for your future objectives.

Additionally, acknowledging accomplishments promotes perseverance in the face of adversity and a positive outlook. It reminds people of their potential and qualities by reorienting the focus from challenges and disappointments to successes and advancement. This optimism strengthens the conviction that objectives can be attained with perseverance and hard work, fostering the will to overcome challenges and endure through trying times.

Celebrate your successes personally but sharing them with others can boost motivation. Telling mentors, coworkers, or supporting communities about your accomplishments and growth can inspire support, guidance, and affirmation. Other people's encouragement and positive comments legitimize efforts and give you more drive to keep moving toward your objectives.

Moreover, sustaining motivation requires regular reflection and goal and strategy revision. Individuals can evaluate what is going well and pinpoint opportunities for growth by reflecting on their progress. It offers a chance to reevaluate objectives, modify schedules, and improve methods in light of changing conditions or fresh information. Long-term motivation maintenance requires flexibility and adaptability since objectives and aspirations can change in response to shifting priorities and life events.

The development of intrinsic motivation is necessary for long-term success and personal growth. An authentic interest in the task at hand, a sense of fulfillment on an individual level, or a deeper meaning and purpose are the sources of intrinsic motivation. One's inherent motivation can be increased by partaking in activities consistent with their values, passions, and strengths, making pursuing goals more gratifying and satisfying.

While they can supplement internal motivation, external motivators like prizes or praise should be utilized sparingly. Although rewards serve as temporary inducements and reinforce positive behavior, excessive dependence on external rewards may eventually reduce intrinsic drive. Maintaining a balance between internal and external motivators helps people stay genuinely committed to their objectives while acknowledging and applauding external successes.

Finally, a growth attitude is critical to staying motivated despite obstacles and failures. According to psychologist Carol Dweck, a growth mindset is the conviction that commitment and diligence can enhance aptitude and intelligence. Resilience and perseverance are fostered by embracing obstacles, growing from setbacks, and seeing them as opportunities for improvement. Those with a development mentality are more likely to remain motivated when faced with challenges because they perceive them as transitory setbacks rather than insurmountable barriers.

To sum up, maintaining motivation is critical to reaching academic, professional, and personal objectives. Setting specific short- and long-term goals, breaking them down into doable tasks, and acknowledging progress are all effective tactics. Long-term motivation maintenance also requires fostering intrinsic motivation, keeping a growth mentality, routinely reviewing accomplishments, and making necessary strategy adjustments. By incorporating these tactics into one's daily routine and mentality, people can improve their ability to bounce back from setbacks and maintain their resolve when pursuing and realizing their goals.

The Role of Patience and Persistence

Speed reading, frequently cited as an essential ability in today's information-rich world, is more than just a method; it is a way of thinking that combines perseverance and patience. Speed reading is a learned skill that needs intentional effort and ongoing improvement, unlike natural aptitudes. This section examines how patience and persistence are essential for learning to read quickly, highlighting the significance of consistent practice for mastery.

Mastering speed reading is not a passive process. It's a journey that requires commitment and perseverance, much like learning to play an instrument or becoming an expert athlete. The first step is to understand the strategies involved—such as reducing subvocalization, increasing peripheral vision, and employing structured reading patterns like skimming and scanning. These strategies aim to balance comprehension and speed, a skill that improves with experience. So, let's dive in and start this active journey towards speed reading mastery.

The ability to be patient is essential for learning how to read quickly. It entails acknowledging that development could be sluggish and that early successes might be small. Mastering rapid reading necessitates overcoming obstacles and failures like any other talent. For example, it can be challenging to break the habit of subvocalization, which involves mentally vocalizing every word as you read. This is because subvocalization is deeply embedded in traditional reading habits. Readers who are patient can overcome their early pain and withstand the want to go back to their old, slower reading habits.

Patience is enhanced by persistence, which provides constant drive and resolve. Becoming proficient in speed reading takes frequent, concentrated practice sessions rather than random practice. Practice consistency creates momentum and reinforces knowledge, progressively increasing reading efficiency and speed. Establishing a program that promotes long-term skill development for speed reading practice involves setting aside a specific time each day or week. This perseverance is essential when things seem to be stagnating or when reading complex texts that take longer to understand at a faster pace.

You must practice often to improve your speed reading abilities and keep up your proficiency over time. Readers must practice purposefully to preserve and enhance their speed reading skills, just as athletes train frequently to maintain optimum performance. In deliberate practice, one focuses on particular aspects of reading technique, such as widening the variety of texts that can be read at increased speeds or improving reading speed without compromising understanding. Through systematic practice sessions, readers may track their development, pinpoint areas for growth, and modify their approach as necessary.

Adding speed reading to everyday activities also makes it more valuable and efficient. Incorporating speed reading into job duties, study sessions, and leisure reading can result in considerable time savings and productivity increases for professionals, students, and lifelong learners. One can efficiently extract meaningful information from reports, academic papers, or fiction books by quickly skimming through them. This frees up time for more in-depth research or other learning activities. Faster reading speed and good comprehension are essential skills in the fast-paced digital society we live in today, where information overload is widespread.

Beyond efficiency, rapid reading also has cognitive benefits, such as increased focus and concentration. Speed reading improves cognitive flexibility and mental agility by teaching the brain to process information more rapidly and efficiently. It improves readers' attentional skills, making it easier to focus through distractions and take in information. These cognitive advantages highlight how crucial it is to practice and persevere to become proficient at speed reading as a talent that improves mental function and learning capacity.

Furthermore, learning to read quickly is a naturally fulfilling experience. Gradually increasing their reading speed and comprehension, readers feel more confident in their skills and can take on more difficult reading. Marking accomplishments—like setting new records for speed reading or mastering the application of skills to various text kinds—reinforces drive and keeps practicing enthusiasts excited. These accomplishments inspire continued skill development and recognize the work required to perfect rapid reading.

In conclusion, developing the skill of rapid reading requires a great deal of patience and perseverance. People can approach learning with patience and accept that development takes time and effort when they understand that fast reading is a learned skill that improves with practice. Because persistence guarantees regular practice and effort, readers can overcome obstacles and gradually improve their speed reading ability. Maintaining and enhancing one's speed reading abilities, incorporating them into daily activities, and reaping the practical and cognitive advantages they provide require consistent effort. In today's information-driven society, people can fully realize the benefits of speed reading and use it as an effective tool for learning, productivity, and personal development by adopting a patient attitude, encouraging perseverance, and making regular practice commitments.

CHAPTER IX

Case Studies and Success Stories

Real-Life Examples of Speed Reading Success

People from all areas of life have adopted speed reading, the art and science of quickly understanding literature, and they have all shown impressive success in their respective fields. These real-world examples from professionals, students, and voracious readers demonstrate how rapid reading can have a profoundly positive impact. We can learn important lessons and takeaways from their experiences, highlighting the potential advantages and real-world uses of this skill.

Anne Jones, a six-time world speed reading champion, is a remarkable example of someone who succeeds at reading quickly. When Anne was a university student, she had to discover more effective ways to manage her workload due to the excessive amount of necessary reading. This is when she developed a need for fast reading. With consistent practice and the use of speed reading strategies, Anne could read much faster without sacrificing her comprehension or recall. This ability has served her well in her academic and professional endeavors, as she has read and retained much knowledge from numerous books. Anne's experience exemplifies how critical speed reading may be for students overburdened with lengthy reading lists and looming deadlines. Her story's most important lesson is how important consistency and practice are. Students can significantly reduce their academic obligations and improve their performance by regularly setting aside time to practice speed reading. This will also help students improve their comprehension and retention.

Another noteworthy one is the incredible tale of Elon Musk, the well-known businessman behind firms like SpaceX and Tesla. Musk is renowned for having an insatiable need for information, and a critical component of his study method has been rapid reading. Musk began reading two novels a day at an early age, a feat made feasible by speed reading. His quick learning curve has dramatically aided his inventive endeavors, allowing him to combine seemingly unrelated subjects and generate ground-breaking concepts. The importance of speed reading for professionals is highlighted by Musk's story, especially for those working in information-intensive, fast-paced fields. The takeaway is that fast reading helps professionals remain ahead of the curve and stimulate creativity by promoting a more profound knowledge of complex material while saving time.

Even voracious readers may attest to the advantages of reading quickly. Every year, Maria Popova, the curator of the well-known blog Brain Pickings, reads hundreds of books and condenses their wisdom into thought-provoking blog entries. Maria's speed reading strategies allow her to efficiently and rapidly read vast amounts of text, which supports her voracious reading habits. Brain Picking is an invaluable resource for readers globally because of her ability to extract and integrate essential concepts from a wide variety of literature. Maria's narrative demonstrates the enjoyment and intellectual stimulation that voracious readers can derive from speed reading. The most important lesson from her experience is that reading quickly can improve a person's capacity to interact with and appreciate literature, expanding their perspectives and understanding.

Overcoming early obstacles and misunderstandings is frequently necessary to become a proficient speed reader. A common misconception is that reading more quickly always results in a decrease in comprehension. However, speed reading techniques aim to improve understanding by teaching the brain to detect and absorb words and sentences more quickly. For example, chunking is a strategy that helps speed up and improve readers' understanding of a text by having them read words in groups rather than one at a time. The habit of silently pronouncing each word while reading, or the technique of reducing subvocalization, can also significantly speed up reading without sacrificing comprehension. Regular practice of these strategies can assist readers in overcoming typical challenges and achieving remarkable reading speeds without sacrificing comprehension.

Success tales on speed reading frequently stress balancing comprehension, and speed is crucial. For instance, productivity hacking enthusiast and author Tim Ferriss has talked about his experience with speed reading. Ferriss supports a systematic approach in which readers modify their reading speed by the intricacy of the content. He advises slowing down when reading dense, complex literature that calls for a deeper understanding and speed reading for lighter, more familiar content. This well-rounded strategy guarantees that readers can effectively consume vast amounts of information while maintaining understanding and critical thinking. Ferriss's experience teaches us that speed reading should be flexible and adaptive, enabling readers to change their reading speed in response to the demands of the content.

Establishing the ideal reading environment is also essential to the success of fast reading. The amount of light, how one stands, and how one reduces distractions are all critical factors that affect reading comprehension and speed. For example, having proper lighting helps lessen eye strain, and having proper posture can help you stay focused and avoid getting tired quickly. Reduced distractions help readers focus and read more efficiently. A few simple strategies to do this include shutting off notifications and making a quiet place to read. These valuable suggestions frequently emphasized in workshops and seminars on speed reading, are crucial for setting up an atmosphere that encourages efficient speed reading. The lesson here is that readers should pay attention to these aspects to maximize their reading experience, as the physical and mental environments are critical to the success of speed reading.

Not only is speed reading a talent, but it's a lifelong process of constant development. Proficient speed readers frequently stress the value of continuous practice and improvement. For instance, Howard Berg, the quickest reader ever recorded by Guinness World Records, credits his accomplishment to a lifetime dedication to reading ability development. Berg shows that mastering fast reading is a continuous process, as he is always looking for new methods and approaches to increase his reading speed and comprehension. His experience serves as a reminder of the value of having a growth mindset and being open to change and education. This experience teaches us that, like any other talent, rapid reading calls for persistence and a commitment to ongoing growth.

In conclusion, the real-world success stories of rapid reading from professionals, students, and voracious readers highlight the significant influence this ability may have on a range of spheres of life. Speed reading has many advantages, including bettering personal intellectual endeavors, fostering professional innovation, and managing academic workloads. The most important lessons to be learned from these tales are the value of consistency and practice, the applicability of speed reading in professional and educational contexts, the advantages of speed reading for cognition, the necessity of a well-rounded strategy, and the importance of setting up an ideal reading environment.

Interviews with Speed Reading Experts

The ability to scan material or speed reading has attracted much attention recently. We seek the advice of fast reading specialists, such as writers, instructors, and researchers, to gain further insight into this intriguing topic. These professionals offer insightful pointers and guidance for becoming proficient in speed reading, clearing up common misconceptions, valuable strategies, and the cognitive advantages of this ability. They do this by drawing on their experiences and expertise.

Tony Buzan, a well-known author and educational consultant who has studied speed reading extensively, is one of the leading experts. Buzan, who created the idea of mind mapping, has studied how the brain interprets information and how to maximize reading speed. Buzan highlights the value of visualizing in speed reading during interviews. He says seeing the text in your mind can significantly improve understanding and recall. Buzan encourages readers to use their imaginations and create vivid mental images while they read. This method not only expedites the reading process but also enhances the retention of the content. His observations demonstrate that rapid reading involves using the brain's visual and associative functions and moving the eyes swiftly across the page.

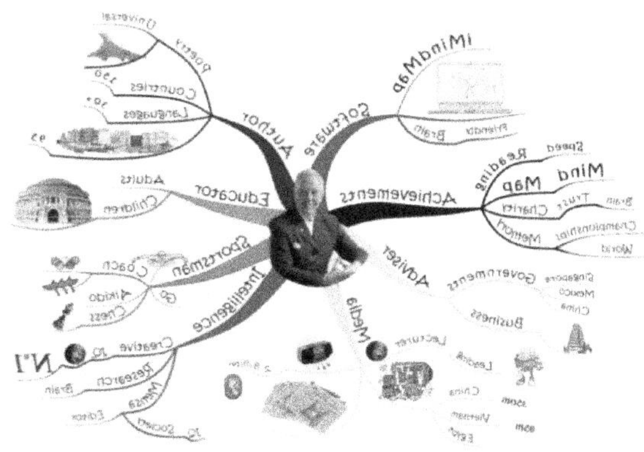

Abby Marks Beale, another well-known name in the subject of speed reading, has written multiple books and created instructional materials to aid in improving readers' efficiency. Beale emphasizes in her interviews the significance of reducing subvocalization and silently pronouncing each word as you read. She argues that because subvocalization restricts the brain's ability to comprehend words at speech rate, it can considerably slow down reading speed. To combat this, Beale advises using strategies like chunking, in which readers arrange words into meaningful clusters to lessen the necessity for subvocalization. She also suggests using a pen or pointer to guide the eyes, which aids concentration and increases reading speed. Beale's guidance emphasizes how important it is to break old patterns and learn new techniques to improve reading efficiency.

Author and entrepreneur Tim Ferriss, well-known for his fascination with efficiency tips, has also talked about his experiences with speed reading. Ferriss promotes the application of the "peripheral vision" technique in his conversations. He clarifies that most readers have a limited focus and frequently overlook the larger context when they read. Readers can read more quickly by learning to use their peripheral vision, allowing them to take in more extensive text passages at a time. Using a sheet of text, Ferriss advises practice by progressively expanding the focus area until the entire line is visible at a look. This method offers a more comprehensive understanding of the material, which speeds up reading and enhances comprehension in general. Ferriss's observations highlight how crucial it is to broaden one's visual horizons to become a more proficient reader.

Keith Rayner, a renowned researcher and cognitive scientist, has significantly contributed to our understanding of how the eyes move during reading. His work sheds important light on how the brain and eyes interact to understand text. Rayner emphasizes the significance of fixation points in interviews—short stop the eyes make to process information. He points out that skilled speed readers can cover more ground faster by reducing the number of fixation sites per line. In addition, Rayner talks about how important it is to minimize regressions or backward eye movements, which can impede reading comprehension and slow reading speed. According to his studies, reading comprehension and speed may be significantly increased by teaching the eyes to move smoothly and efficiently across the text. Rayner's work highlights the scientific basis of speed reading methods and their ability to maximize reading efficiency.

Organizations and training courses devoted to advancing speed reading abilities exist in addition to loan specialists. Millions of people utilize the well-known speed reading program that industry pioneer Evelyn Wood created. Interviews with Evelyn Wood Reading Dynamics program instructors reveal several essential tactics for efficient speed reading. Using a hand or a pointer to lead their gaze across the text is a tactic known as "meta-guiding." This method lessens distractions and aids in maintaining a steady reading pace. To monitor improvement, instructors also stress the value of consistent practice and the establishment of small goals. These observations demonstrate that fast reading is a talent that may be enhanced by regular training and organized instruction.

Researchers are also interested in the cognitive advantages of rapid reading. Cognitive neuroscientist Dr. Stanislas Dehaene has studied the neuronal circuits in the brain about reading. According to Dehaene in his interviews, speed reading can improve cognitive flexibility, or the brain's capacity to transition between various tasks and mental processes. He points out that proficient speed readers frequently show enhanced critical thinking, memory, and attention spans. Reading quickly helps the brain establish stronger neural connections by rapidly processing information. Dehaene's research supports speed reading's cognitive benefits scientifically, which also suggests that speed reading might be a valuable tool for mental agility and lifetime learning.

Speed reading has many advantages, but there are drawbacks and myths. One prevalent misperception is that reading quickly causes comprehension to suffer. Experts counter that this is only sometimes the case, though. When fast reading methods are used correctly, understanding can increase, according to psychologist and speed reading expert Dr. Marc Seifer. Seifer suggests in his interviews that readers begin with well-known content and progressively increase the difficulty level as their speed increases. This systematic approach guarantees knowledge and fosters trust. Seifer's observations emphasize that mastering speed and comprehension with repetition and persistence is necessary for proficient speed reading.

Experts frequently point out that staying focused and concentrated when reading quickly might be challenging. Learning Strategies Corporation co-founder Dr. Paul Scheele discusses this problem in his interviews. He recommends adding mindfulness exercises to the fast-reading curriculum. Deep breathing and visualization are two methods that help clear the mind and increase focus. To prevent mental exhaustion and preserve peak performance, Scheele also suggests taking regular pauses. His guidance emphasizes mental readiness and calm to succeed at fast reading.

In conclusion, interviews with professionals in the field of fast reading offer a plethora of knowledge about the methods, difficulties, and advantages of this ability. Some authors, like Tim Ferriss and Tony Buzan, promote peripheral vision, while others, like Abby Marks Beale, stress the value of imagery and limiting subvocalization. Scholars such as Dr. Stanislas Dehaene and Keith Rayner emphasize the benefits of fast reading for cognition and its scientific foundation. Experts contend that contrary to popular belief, practice and the correct methods can improve comprehension and speed when it comes to speed reading. Combining technology and mindfulness techniques can also enhance the speed reading experience. These professional pointers and recommendations highlight the importance of speed reading as a skill that can be honed and improved, providing a wealth of career and personal development advantages.

Applying Lessons to Your Own Journey

Anyone who wants to improve their reading efficiency can benefit greatly from learning the speed reading ability, which enables readers to read and comprehend content more quickly. These techniques can be customized to build a unique speed reading schedule by reviewing case studies and professional assistance. This section will examine how to incorporate practical strategies, apply knowledge from proficient speed readers, and create a tailored plan that meets specific objectives.

Knowing the fundamental strategies effective speed readers use is the first step in developing a customized speed reading plan. Minimizing subvocalization—silently speaking each word while reading—is one such strategy. The reading speed can be considerably reduced by using this method. Renowned speed reader Abby Marks Beale advises readers to break this behavior by practicing chunking or assembling words into meaningful clusters. For example, practice reading in phrases or groups of three to four words rather than one word at a time. This helps with comprehension and speed because it enables the brain to handle more information simultaneously.

To become proficient in speed reading, practice must be incorporated into daily activities regularly. The secret to mastering and retaining this ability is consistency. Allocate a specific period every day to practice speed reading. Set small, achievable objectives at first, like reading for ten to fifteen minutes each day, and as your skills advance, progressively extend the time. Reading various things, such as books, articles, and reports, can foster flexibility and versatility in many settings.

A vital element of any successful speed reading program is personalization. Everybody has different reading habits, talents, and shortcomings. For this reason, it's critical to modify the plan to meet individual needs and objectives. Start by evaluating your present understanding and reading speed. Apps and web resources tracking reading speed and offering feedback can be used. Setting reasonable and attainable goals will be easier if you know your baseline performance.

One helpful strategy is making a reading schedule that fits your everyday routine. When you are most attentive and concentrated throughout the day, note these times and plan your speed reading exercise around them. Set aside time for reading practice after breakfast, for example, if you discover you are more productive in the morning. On the other hand, if you are a night owl, you might practice after work. You can increase the efficiency of your practice sessions by modifying the calendar to match your innate rhythms.

An additional crucial component of a customized speed reading program is progress tracking. Maintaining a journal of reading comprehension, pace, and material selection might give you important information about how you've improved over time. Establish quantifiable, precise objectives. For example, raise your reading speed to a particular word per minute or your comprehension score to a specific percentage. You can find areas for development and modify your practice tactics by regularly analyzing your progress.

Including cognitive activities in your speed reading regimen might help improve your reading comprehension. In addition to speed reading practice, methods like memory exercises, critical thinking exercises, and visualization can enhance understanding and retention. For instance, pause to picture the critical concepts after reading a section and conjure up visuals in your mind. By doing so, the information may be reinforced and become more memorable. Similarly, engaging in memory exercises that involve jotting down essential details from the book will improve comprehension and retention.

You can use technology as a valuable friend to advance your speed reading skills. Many applications and software packages are available to facilitate practice with speed reading, providing interactive drills, progress monitoring, and customized training regimens. Through planned activities, guided reading programs such as Spreeder and Spritz assist users in improving their reading comprehension and speed. You can regularly incorporate these tools into your practice sessions to improve your success by getting extra help and feedback.

You must have perseverance and patience as you progress with your speed reading. Acquiring proficiency in rapid reading is a progressive process that involves commitment and hard work. Recognize and appreciate your little accomplishments along the road, and don't let failure deter you. Remember that improving general understanding and retention is the main objective, not merely reading more quickly. You can significantly increase the effectiveness of your reading by being dedicated to your practice and continually improving your methods.

In conclusion, developing a customized speed reading plan based on needs and objectives can be facilitated by incorporating expert guidance and lessons from successful speed readers. Essential tactics include reducing subvocalization, keeping focus with a guide, increasing peripheral vision, and setting up a comfortable reading space. An effective plan must include personalization, progress tracking, and consistent practice. You may improve your speed reading even more by using technology and adding cognitive workouts. If you are persistent and patient, you may learn speed reading and take advantage of its many advantages for professional and personal development.

CHAPTER X

Next Steps To Speed Reading

Recap of Key Concepts

Speed reading, a potent tool for improving reading effectiveness, includes a range of methods and approaches intended to raise reading speed without compromising understanding. This section summarizes the main ideas discussed in speed reading, outlines the most essential strategies and techniques, and considers the advancements and successes that can be obtained with consistent practice.

Minimizing subvocalization—silently pronouncing each word as you read—is one of the core strategies of fast reading. Although this technique is natural, it restricts reading speed to 150–250 words per minute, which is the speed of speech. To increase reading speed, experts like Abby Marks Beale stress the need to conquer subvocalization. Reading phrases rather than words allows the brain to digest information more quickly. One technique that helps with this is chunking, when readers arrange words into meaningful clusters. This technique improves speed and understanding by allowing readers to process longer material passages simultaneously.

Meta-guidance, which entails guiding the eyes along the text's lines using a pointer—a finger or a pen, for example—is another crucial tactic. This method reduces distractions and aids in maintaining a steady reading pace. This technique was made known by fast reading pioneer Evelyn Wood through her Reading Dynamics curriculum. Meta-guiding lessens the propensity to regress or go back, which can impede reading comprehension and cause reading speed to decrease.

Readers can focus better and read more steadily by employing a guide necessary for efficient reading.

Increasing one's field of view is another essential element of rapid reading. Tim Ferriss, a proponent of productivity methods, suggests teaching the eyes to process more material simultaneously. Most readers can only process a certain quantity of text at a time due to their restricted focal point. Readers' reading speed can be significantly increased by expanding this concentration area. Readers can gradually expand their concentration region until they can read complete lines at a glance by practicing with a text sheet. By offering a more comprehensive understanding of the text, this approach expedites the reading process and improves comprehension overall.

Another crucial component of efficient speed reading is setting up the right environment for reading. Adequate lighting, cozy sitting, and a peaceful, distraction-free environment are some elements that can significantly affect reading productivity. Keith Rayner, a cognitive scientist, emphasizes the significance of limiting outside distractions to sustain attention and lessen eye strain. While a cozy and peaceful setting aids in maintaining focus and discourages fatigue, well-lit areas enable readers to practice speed reading more successfully.

To become proficient in speed reading, you must practice frequently. Over time, performance improves, and techniques become more solidified with consistent, focused practice. Significant gains can be achieved by scheduling dedicated daily periods for practicing speed reading. Building endurance and expertise can be facilitated by starting with short, reasonable sessions and progressively lengthening them as proficiency increases. Diverse reading materials, such as books, articles, and reports, can aid in developing flexibility and adaptability in various settings.

Customization is essential to a successful speed reading strategy. Since every person is different in terms of their strengths, limitations, and reading preferences, it is crucial to customize a speed reading program to meet individual needs and objectives. Setting reasonable and doable goals starts with determining reading comprehension and speed levels. Monitoring development with reading speed, comprehension, and content type records can yield important insights into how well one is improving over time. Maintaining motivation and focus can be facilitated by setting concrete, quantifiable goals, such as raising comprehension scores or reading more words per minute.

A fast reading program that includes cognitive exercises can further improve reading comprehension. In addition to speed reading drills, visualization, memory tests, and critical thinking exercises can enhance understanding and retention. For instance, after reading a section, visualizing the key ideas and forming mental images of the content might help to reinforce and improve memory of the information. Reading can be made more efficient by engaging in memory exercises, such as repeating essential passages from the text, which can improve comprehension and retention.

Technology is also an excellent tool for improving one's fast reading abilities. Many applications and software packages, including Spritz and Spreeder, offer personalized training regimens, progress tracking, and interactive exercises. Through planned exercises, these technologies assist users in improving their reading comprehension and speed by providing real-time feedback and guided reading practice. Adding these resources into regular practice sessions may give you more encouragement and feedback, improving your development and the general efficiency of your speed reading instruction.

A crucial component of the journey towards rapid reading is introspection about advancements and successes. Becoming an expert reader quickly is a gradual process that takes commitment and work. Recognizing little accomplishments and turning points into opportunities for growth promotes motivation and ongoing progress. It's critical to remember that the purpose of speed reading is to improve comprehension and retention in addition to reading more quickly. Significant gains in reading efficiency can be made by regularly practicing and enhancing methods.

To sum up, speed reading is a valuable talent that includes a variety of methods and approaches intended to improve reading comprehension and speed. The essential ideas are to minimize subvocalization, apply meta-guiding, increase peripheral vision, and set up the ideal reading environment. An effective speed reading plan must include personalization, progress tracking, and consistent practice. Reading skills can be further improved by utilizing technology and including cognitive activities. Maintaining motivation and promoting continual growth is facilitated by reviewing progress and acknowledging accomplishments. People can learn speed reading and take advantage of its many advantages for professional and personal development by implementing these tactics and ideas.

Creating a Long-Term Speed Reading Plan

Developing a long-term speed reading plan is imperative for anyone hoping to utilize this critical talent fully. Speed reading increases comprehension and retention while increasing the efficiency with which information is absorbed. Setting long-term objectives, creating benchmarks, and implementing methods are all part of a well-organized plan to sustain and improve speed reading abilities over time. This section overviews the essential elements of developing a long-term, substantial speed reading program.

A good speed reading strategy begins with well-defined, attainable objectives. These objectives ought to be SMART—specific, measurable, achievable, relevant, and time-bound. One possible starting point could be to read 50 words per minute (wpm) more during the first month of the challenge. One of the following aims could be to reach 500 words per minute while keeping or raising understanding. Such goals give focus and inspiration, facilitating progress monitoring and plan adherence.

Milestones are essential to a long-term strategy for fast reading. They act as checkpoints to monitor development and ensure the objectives are reached. Accomplishments in both comprehension and speed may determine milestones. For instance, reducing subvocalization and learning to read in chunks during the first two weeks could be considered early milestones. Acquiring proficiency in using a guiding instrument, such as a pen or finger, to aid in sustaining reading speed and lessen regression could be another benchmark. These little successes contribute to self-assurance and a feeling of achievement, which are necessary for maintaining long-term effort.

Incorporating frequent practice into everyday activities is critical to preserving and improving speed reading abilities. Reinforcing new reading habits and skills requires consistency. Allocate a specific period every day for practicing speed reading. This could start as little as ten to fifteen minutes and then increase as you get accustomed to the methods. Practice speed reading during these exercises, including limiting regressions, employing a guide, and improving your peripheral vision. Increasing the variety of reading resources you use, including books, papers, and articles, can also aid in the skills' adaptation to different content types and settings.

An effective long-term speed reading program must include both self-evaluation and feedback. Testing your comprehension and reading speed regularly gives you essential information about where you're at and where you still need to develop. Many web resources and applications are available for assessing reading comprehension and speed. These programs can track your development over time and offer immediate feedback. Reviewing this feedback, you can focus your practice sessions on areas where you are having trouble and hone practical approaches.

Cognitive activities are a great way to improve your speed reading abilities. Practice reading quickly is enhanced by visualization, memory-boosting, and critical thinking exercises. Visualizing the text can improve comprehension and recall by forming mental images of it. Recalling important details or summarizing the material after reading are memory exercises that can strengthen retention. Engaging in critical thinking exercises that evaluate and challenge the content can help improve understanding and retention.

One cannot undervalue the contribution of technology to the preservation and improvement of rapid reading abilities. Numerous software applications and apps are available to help with speed reading practice. Programs like Spreeder and Spritz provide interactive workouts, progress monitoring, and individualized training regimens. These tools can offer adaptive exercises and real-time feedback based on your goals and reading ability. You can spice up and strengthen your speed reading journey by incorporating these tools into your regular practice regimen.

Setting up a comfortable reading space is crucial for efficient speed reading. Adequate lighting, cozy sitting, and a peaceful, distraction-free environment are some elements that can significantly affect reading productivity. Longer practice sessions are made possible by comfortable seating arrangements and well-lit surroundings that reduce eye strain and tiredness. Reducing disturbances and noise will help you focus and concentrate, which is essential while practicing speed reading strategies.

Mindfulness and relaxation practices can also greatly enhance one's reading ability. Visualization, meditation, and deep breathing can help lower tension and increase focus. Before using brief mindfulness activities can aid focus and calm the mind before or during reading periods. These routines can improve general cognitive health and are particularly helpful for sustaining focus during extended reading sessions.

Motivation must be maintained for a long-term speed reading program to be successful. Additional incentives can be obtained by establishing immediate and long-term rewards for reaching milestones and objectives. Rewarding oneself with a favorite pastime or a treat after hitting a specific goal could be as easy as taking a break. Joining a group of other fast readers or sharing your accomplishments with friends can also help and inspire you. Learning can be made more fun and motivational through social contact and shared experiences.

A long-term speed reading plan should include reflection on accomplishments and growth. Reviewing your progress regularly will help you determine which tactics are effective and which require modification. Recording your practice sessions in a journal and documenting your progress, difficulties, and tactics might yield insightful information. Additionally, reflection aids in goal-setting and goal-adjustment based on your achievements. Honoring accomplishments, no matter how modest, can increase self-esteem and strengthen the resolve to improve.

To sum up, developing a long-term strategy for speed reading entails defining precise objectives, setting benchmarks, and putting techniques for consistent practice, criticism, and self-evaluation into practice. Maintaining and improving fast reading abilities requires incorporating cognitive exercises, using technology, and setting up a comfortable reading space. The journey can be further supported by mindfulness exercises, incentives, and social contact to sustain motivation. Regular reflection on advancements and accomplishments ensures long-term success and continual growth. Speed reading can be a valuable skill for professional and personal development with perseverance and dedication, allowing for the quick and efficient assimilation of knowledge.

Encouragement and Final Thoughts

Starting the path to learning rapid reading is an ambitious and gratifying goal. It shows a commitment to improving one's ability to absorb information and instilling a lifelong passion for learning. As we end our investigation into speed reading, it is critical to consider the motivational factors that can prolong this journey and the broader benefits of developing a habit of continual learning and reading.

Speed reading is more than just a technique for faster processing of words; it is a gateway to more efficient knowledge access and engagement with a broader range of material. The ability to read rapidly and comprehend effectively creates new opportunities for personal and professional development. Imagine being able to keep up with the latest research in your profession, read classic literature, remain current on current events, and study various topics in a fraction of the time it used to take. This skill can significantly improve your competence, broaden your ideas, and help to a more balanced intellectual existence.

However, mastering speed reading takes time, patience, and practice. It is a skill that improves over time, with each step forward resulting in noticeable gains in speed and comprehension. Maintaining an optimistic and resilient mindset is critical, particularly when confronted with setbacks or plateaus in progress. Remember, every master was once a beginner. The first hardships and small successes are all part of the learning experience. Accept these instances as opportunities to improve and develop your techniques.

One of the most compelling parts of speed reading is seeing concrete results. As you practice regularly, you will see increases in your reading speed and knowledge retention. These modest triumphs are essential reminders of your ability to learn and adapt. Celebrate these milestones, no matter how minor they appear. Each achievement demonstrates your dedication and work, providing further inspiration to continue on this path.

Furthermore, speed reading is ideally aligned with the idea of lifelong learning. In today's fast changing environment, the capacity to constantly learn new things and abilities is vital. Lifelong learning stimulates the mind, improves professional skills, and creates a more profound view of the world. Speed reading provides the tools to traverse this trip more efficiently, allowing you to quickly absorb new knowledge and stay ahead in your personal and professional pursuits.

Beyond the practical benefits, fast reading improves your intellectual life. Books are portals to other planets, cultures, and ideas. They provide insights into human experiences, helpful knowledge, and encourage creativity and critical thinking. You can read more books and articles by improving your speed reading skills, broadening your horizons, and enriching your intellectual and emotional life. The thrill of discovering new authors, exploring other genres, and delving into complex topics becomes more accessible, making reading a more fascinating and rewarding hobby.

Furthermore, rapid reading has a significant impact on your work life. In many professions, remaining updated and current with the latest advances is critical. Quickly processing and interpreting massive amounts of information can provide a competitive advantage. Speed reading can help you stay on top of industry trends, read papers and proposals, and research more efficiently and productively. This talent can help you make better judgments, contribute more effectively to your team, and succeed in your profession.

In addition to professional benefits, fast reading promotes personal development. It cultivates a sense of curiosity and inquiry, motivating you to seek out new information and experiences. This habit can lead to a more enriching and meaningful life because you always discover new hobbies and passions. Learning and growing becomes a lifelong adventure full of joy and discovery. As a result, speed reading becomes a tool for learning and improving your general quality of life.

As you improve your speed reading abilities, try to keep the joy of reading alive. While the goal is to read more effectively, it's critical to maintain sight of the enjoyment that reading provides. Select materials that intrigue and inspire you. Allow yourself to become immersed in a good tale or charmed by amazing facts. This mix of efficiency and enjoyment ensures that reading remains a pleasurable and rewarding experience.

Finally, becoming a skilled speed reader is a rewarding endeavor with multiple advantages. It improves your ability to assimilate information rapidly, encourages lifelong learning, broadens your intellectual and emotional life, and gives you a competitive advantage in your professional career. It is a skill that demands devotion and practice, but the benefits outweigh the effort.

Stay motivated by acknowledging your accomplishments and welcoming difficulties along the way. Remember that every step forward, no matter how tiny, gets you closer to your objective. Keep the pleasure of reading at the forefront of your efforts and let your curiosity and want to learn guide you. Speed reading is more than simply an efficiency tool; it is a way to connect more intimately with the world of knowledge and ideas.

Encourage yourself to continue learning and progressing through fast reading or other educational activities. Lifelong learning is a journey that enhances both your mind and spirit, with limitless possibilities for discovery and progress. Integrating speed reading into your life empowers you to take advantage of these chances and reach your best potential.

Accept this adventure with excitement and an open mind, and you will discover that fast reading is a valuable ally in your search for knowledge and self-improvement. The skills and knowledge you gain will benefit your personal and professional lives and contribute to a better understanding and appreciation for the world around you.

CONCLUSION

As we conclude "Speed Reading: Unlock Your Brain's Potential: Master the Art of Speed Reading and Boost Your Learning Efficiency," it's a moment to celebrate the transformative journey you've embarked upon. Setting attainable goals, creating an optimal reading environment, and consistently practicing the abilities you've acquired will put you on the way to becoming a skilled speed reader, demonstrating your growth and empowerment.

Speed reading is not just a skill; it's a gateway to unlocking your brain's full potential. Whether you're tackling academic texts, professional reports, or leisurely novels, the ability to read quickly and efficiently enables you to absorb more information in less time, significantly enhancing your overall learning efficiency. The cognitive strategies and advanced techniques outlined in this book not only boost your reading speed, but also enhance your retention and comprehension, giving you a competitive edge in your learning journey.

Always remember that mastery requires patience and persistence. Take pride in every step of your progress, no matter how small, and continue to challenge yourself. The real-life success stories and expert insights shared in this book are a testament to what can be achieved with dedication and the right approach.

Accept lifelong learning, remain interested, and allow the abilities you've gained here to propel you toward even more excellent knowledge and achievement. Your journey does not end here; it is simply the start of a new, empowered way of reading and learning.

Thank you for buying and reading/ listening to our book. If you found this book useful/ helpful please take a few minutes and leave a review on the platform where you purchased our book. Your feedback matters greatly to us.